THE P⊙WER OF PURP⊙SED PERFORMANCE

Choosing to Live Your Life on Purpose

Allen Tappe

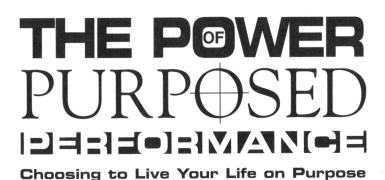

**Institute for
Purposed Performance**SM
Helping people choose.

Arlington, Texas

www.TappeGroup.com

The Power of Purposed Performance:
Choosing to Live Your Life on Purpose
Copyright © 2003 Allen Tappe

Published by the Institute for Purposed Performance^{SM}
817-226-1170
www.TappeGroup.com

Editor: Patty Crowley
Designer: Jan Blanchard

ISBN: 0-9724-5762-3
03 04 05 06 07   5 4 3 2 1

To Barbara,
my wife, my love, and my best friend

and

To Angela, Jill, and Meredith,
my daughters, my treasure, and my joy

because He lives.

TEN CHOICES YOU WILL LEARN TO MAKE AS A PURPOSED PERFORMER:

1. Choose to be a leader, on purpose.

2. Decide not to be a victim.

3. Accept personal responsibility for your choices.

4. Respond. Don't react.

5. Know your reason why.

6. Believe in your personal distinction.

7. Recognize and value the people on your life team.

8. Respect and embrace conflict.

9. Listen more and talk less.

10. Keep expectations clarified.

An important element of Purposed Performance is maintaining a positive attitude. To help you do that, focus on the Affirmations at the end of chapters 3-14. Repeat them to yourself, out loud if possible.

Log on to **www.TappeGroup.com** for a complete, compiled listing of the Affirmations and for information about the Tappe Group or Purposed Performance^{SM}.

CONTENTS

BEFORE
YOU BEGIN

Writing this book has been both a blessing and a challenge for me. It has been a blessing in that it has afforded me the opportunity to reflect upon the people who have been so instrumental in my life and the moments we have shared. On the other hand, it has been an incredible challenge. I had to first become convinced this book needed to be written. So many people have contributed to the things I think I know. They are the ones who truly author this book. People I respect have encouraged me to give written life to Purposed Performance℠. Because of their affirmation, I have come to believe in this project. Because I am the only one who has seen life through the eyes of my heart, I am the only one who can provide the reflections they have encouraged. What you are about to read is what I believe. It is what I have seen. It is how I attempt to live.

—Allen Tappe

INTRODUCTION

LIVING WITH
CONVICTION

Are you tired of having life happen to you? Tired of knowing the things to do but never quite getting them done? Are you weary of making excuses and blaming others for not meeting your challenges? Are you fed up playing the role of victim? If so, this book is for you.

Positive personal growth is not a natural experience. It is something you have to do on purpose. Doing something on purpose requires conviction. Otherwise, you leave it undone because it's easier. Doing life on purpose is definitely not the easy way to go. Many don't believe it is possible.

I've been privileged to work with people throughout this world who epitomize purposed living. They face some of life's most significant challenges, and yet they will not allow themselves to be made a victim of their circumstances. What is the difference between those who overcome and those who let life happen to them? This book is a tribute to those who model the power of purposed living and clearly represent the answer to the question.

Several years ago, I met a young woman who came to me for personal coaching. She wanted to be a professional speaker. What got my attention immediately was the fact that Paige was challenged with cerebral palsy. She had been since birth. Yet, I have never met a more vibrant and positive person in my life. She had just graduated from college, received national recognition for her work as an equestrian, and just happened to be on her way to ski. I asked Paige if there was anything she couldn't do, and she told me she didn't play basketball very well. She smiled and told me she understood her limitations. By the way, she was already a professional speaker. She speaks to thousands of people in an attempt to encourage those who share her challenge. She has chosen not to be a victim, and as a result, the world around her is being changed.

One of the most influential people in my life was a man who began his professional life as a farmer. Bill was a rather shy and unassuming man with more power in his character than anyone I have ever known. Although all forces pointed to the farm, Bill decided to pursue a different course. With the support of his wife and family, he moved to the city and became an insurance professional, selling for a living. The reason he chose sales as his course was because it provided him the freedom to really live life with conviction. Although it was totally contrary to his basically shy nature, he knew it would provide him the freedom to be with his children when they needed him. He would also have quality time with his life partner. He and Joy built an exceptional family and a marriage that literally lasted a lifetime. Once I tried to encourage Bill to pursue a rather large corporate account where I had some influence. It would have meant a lot more money for him and even greater recognition as a professional. I'll never forget what he told me. He said he would have to pass because taking that account would force him to do some things he was not prepared to do, namely steal some of the freedom he had worked to create for himself. Then, I could not understand. Now, I can. Bill knew what he wanted, and he purposed to have it. He would not be victimized even by the prospect of greater success. Bill was my father-in-law. In many ways, he was also my hero. Even in death, Bill was unwilling to be the victim. Facing pancreatic cancer, he decided to leave this world on his terms. Quality of life was more important to him than a few more days of being debilitated by the effects of massive chemotherapy. He went home to be with his family. He went home to die with his family. He ultimately went home to be with his God. And he did it on purpose.

The first real mentor I had in my life was my tennis coach. As a sophomore in high school, my first impression of him was not very positive. In fact, I thought he was a little nuts. On the first day of practice, he told us to meet him in a classroom and leave our racquets behind. He came into the room and began to explain to us the gaggle, the relationship of geese in flight. He drew on the board the pattern they created. He explained the relationship they maintained as they flew. He then told us we'd be reading Plato's *Republic*. As a teenager, I thought he was crazy. As an adult, I now know just how wise he was and just how fortunate I was. Cal wanted us to understand the power of team. Even in an individual sport like tennis, he wanted us to experience the dynamic relationship of people working together toward a common goal with a common vision. He held us to high standards of behavior and performance. The experience was life changing and life shaping for me. Cal could have done anything he wanted to do. He was, and is, a talented and gifted man. He was a three-sport athlete in college. He played professional baseball and taught golf. He could have coached college tennis for a prestigious university, but he chose to coach high school tennis. He did it on purpose. For thirty years he influenced and changed the lives of high school athletes. I was blessed to have been one of them.

What makes the difference? What sets these people apart? I believe it is their conviction. They embrace life with purpose and passion because they are moving with and through their convictions. This book is about doing life on purpose. As a result, it is about conviction. More specifically, it is about putting your convictions into motion. Through my work with people, I have come to believe the reason we don't get more done in life is because we don't understand how it works. We think because we decide to change a life-long habit one day, it is just going to happen. We underestimate what is involved in living life on purpose. As a result, we stay frustrated with what we regard as failure, and many times we just give up the fight. This book is meant to help you both understand the convictions essential to purposed living in the twenty-first century and recognize the steps, or progression, essential to embracing these convictions. My hope is that through this project you will be inspired and encouraged to become the purposed performer you long to be. Your response will be a tribute to Paige and Bill and Cal and all of the people who have inspired you and me to keep growing forward.

Purposed Performance^{SM}
Progression

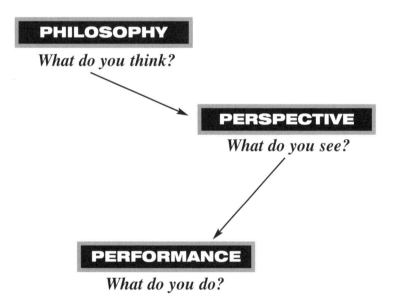

PHILOSOPHY
What do you think?

PERSPECTIVE
What do you see?

PERFORMANCE
What do you do?

PURPOSED
PERFORMANCE
PROGRESSION

How do things work in your life? How do you get from one point to the next? Have you ever thought about it? In order to have any sense of purpose in your life, you have to first become a student of how you work. In the process, you will come to better understand the people around you. Everyone has an approach to facing life and its challenges whether we realize it or not. We all have an operating system for performance in life. At the heartbeat of that operating system will be a progression. This book is about your coming to a deeper understanding of how you work. Understanding the presence of this progression in your life is the first step toward understanding you. Purposed Performance℠ is an operating system for life that flows through a purposed progression. You are the only one who can alter the flow of this progression in your life.

PHILOSOPHY: WHAT YOU THINK

I had the opportunity a few years ago to work with a dentist who had the unfortunate distinction of experiencing staff turnover, almost completely, twice per year. He was so frustrated that he had determined to leave the profession if things did not change. I had dinner with him the evening before we were to meet with his staff, and I listened to all of his frustrations. After dinner, I told him that the fix for his frustration was going to be easier than I had expected. In fact, I suggested that he really did not need me at all. He simply needed to go into the meeting the next day and tell them all that he would no longer need their services. I suggested that he be fair with them in the process, yet at the same time be clear about his decision. I further recommended that he call his landlord and negotiate a new lease based upon a substantially reduced office size. I encouraged him to have a very small office with just enough room for himself and his patients. He finally spoke up and said, "Have you lost your mind?"

I said, "No, we've fixed your staff problem. You now don't have one. You are on your own."

To which he responded, "I need those people."

I then was able to say, "Now we are ready to begin." You see, this dentist was great with his patients because he knew how much he needed them. He had a hard time with his staff because he did not think about just how much he needed them. I am pleased to say that he had an "a-ha" experience, and the last time I checked he was having great success with his staff.

No one can believe for you. No one can dream for you.

To be a purposed performer, you need to begin with your own heart and mind. You have to begin with what you think about life and all of its challenges. The first step in life's progression is your ***philosophy***. It all begins with you and what you think and believe—with what you dream. No one can believe for you. No one can dream for you. Everything you face in life will be defined by your own personal belief system. As a result, it is vital for you to be in touch with yourself and your personal philosophy for living.

To begin with, you have to accept responsibility for what you believe. You can't blame anyone for what you allow to occupy your heart and mind. Many people passively accept the belief system of their parents as though it is something that can be inherited. Others are controlled by the thoughts of people around them. You cannot allow your personal philosophy to be someone else's production. To the degree you live life through the philosophy of others, you are living life for someone else. The exciting thing about a personal belief system is that it is something you can and should produce for yourself. The question is, What life philosophy do you choose?

Your philosophy should provide the solid foundation you need to face life's challenges. In the process of creating your philosophy, there are three specific questions that you must ask yourself. Your answers to them will provide the spiritual and emotional foundation you will need for living a purposed life.

1. Who are you? This first question is simple yet probably the most profound question in life. Because the real issue is one of identity, another way to ask might be, How do you define yourself? What kind of relationship do you have with *you*? Any personal belief system will spring from the way you see yourself fitting into the world. Your attitude concerning responsibility and accountability will flow from your philosophy about you.

Much has been written and said on the subject of self-image. My purpose here is to make sure you realize just how dramatically what you believe about yourself impacts how you deal with you. Doing life on purpose will be difficult if you see yourself as an accident. My encourage-

Choose a life philosophy that celebrates you as a unique creation.

ment is for you to choose a life philosophy that celebrates you as a unique creation. In a very real sense, you get to choose who you are going to be and what you are going to become. What you choose to believe is personal to you and must originate within you. Don't settle for a self-defining philosophy that does not respect who you are. If you do, all your life will be approached from that vantage point. If you have no respect for yourself, no one else will either. You have to believe you are worthy!

Too many children have been misled to believe they have no value because of the destructive conflict between a mother and a father. Too many wives/husbands have been left to conclude they were not good enough because of a mate's choice of another partner. Too many employees have been destroyed by a corporate decision to downsize. The list could go on and on. Countless people have been victims of the dysfunction, deceitfulness, or decision of another person. Your life philosophy must be strong enough to bear up under the weight of others. You cannot afford to let life and its challenges define you. You must face life with a clear sense of identity that is noncontingent. You must define the world through your system of thought, not theirs, if you are going to live a purposed life.

Too often we allow circumstances, particularly tragedies, of life to define us. Cynthia is a woman who dramatically exemplifies the negative consequence of allowing life to define us. For more than a decade of her life as a young woman, she was victimized by the self-inflicted punishment of bulimia. Her addiction to the behavior almost killed her. Fortunately, for her and for our world, she found help. Through therapy she discovered that for years she had defined herself as "damaged goods" because of an unfortunate accident she had as a small child. As an adult, she still saw herself through the eyes of a hurting, guilty, and frightened child. She tells her story in her book, *The Monster Within*, and has spent her life as the founder of the National Bulimic Foundation, helping people find freedom from similar bondage. When you don't let people, life, or your perceptions about life define you, you can succeed!

2. What is your purpose in life? This significant question concerning your philosophy has to do with *what* you do. The issue here is about your perceived significance. Do you believe you make any difference in this life? Do you believe each day you have a specific and special reason to live? Choices you make about how to live life will flow from your philosophy of life. The quality of your daily performance will be a product of the passion you feel toward the things you are doing. The attitude you have about what you do each day will in many ways be impacted by the significance you attach to it.

I once had an unexpected learning opportunity while traveling through the Orlando airport on my way to a speaking engagement. Because of the number of bags Barbara and I had between us, I found a young man to help us. While he was pleasant, he was not overwhelming with his customer service. I honestly didn't expect much more out of him, and I couldn't help but notice another guy who had a much more difficult challenge than our guy had. He was trying to take care of the baggage for a rather large group of women. Not that because they were women added anything to his challenge. He had more to do than he could handle. Yet, he had this big smile on his face, and was so positive and reassuring. I had to find the secret to this refreshing approach to his job. His name was Carl. I asked him to help me understand what gave him such an upbeat approach to dealing with challenging situations. He said, "That's easy . . . I have the greatest job in the world!" I have to tell you, it was hard for me to believe this "baggage guy" at the airport could think his job was the greatest in the world. I asked him to explain. He said, "I get to meet and welcome people from all over the world. I get to encourage them and help them a little along their way." Carl is an example of a guy whose life philosophy gives him a reason to live every day. It gives him a sense of purpose. And as a result, he embraces life with passion and a genuine sense of significance.

3. How secure do you feel each day as you face life? This final question for your philosophical puzzle has to do with your sense of security. How much does life around you determine just how secure you feel? No doubt about it, life is fickle. You simply can't look outside of yourself to find security. It no longer can be found in the companies you work for. We are living in a time when, if your company can do without you, they will! No longer can you find security in the person you have chosen as your life partner. They may decide to leave and find another partner for life. People you love may die, in spite of all of your best efforts. Your security cannot be found in your children, because they are going to grow up and leave home. You cannot afford to place your security in what you think you know, because it could all change tomorrow. I don't know of a single industry not facing major redefinition.

After 9-11, you can no longer feel secure in any normal situation. You can't afford to place your security in your heritage because it is also subject to change.

If your security is based on being an American, what would happen if America went away? Years ago, while I was living in the Republic of South Africa, I had the opportunity to see firsthand how a redefined nation can affect the lives of people. We lived in the northern part of the country, and therefore had many who immigrated into the Republic from what was then Rhodesia.

As a result of the tragic war fought in that country, many were displaced from their homes, never to return. They were escorted to the border and given a thousand dollars. Their property was nationalized. They were now a people without a home. One of those people was a woman I came to know. When I met her, she was totally despondent and had given up on life. In fact, her husband was facing the real prospect of having her hospitalized. As we met together, it became clear to me she was suffering from a total lack of identity. As a result, she also suffered from incredible fear and insecurity. She was paralyzed because she no longer had clarity about life. She was no longer a Rhodesian. The country had been redefined. It was and is now, Zimbabwe. She could no longer depend upon her heritage because it seemed to have been *People who* misplaced. She and I spent much time together discussing *live life on* the reality of who she was and what she depended on for her *purpose don't* security. She had to make some philosophical choices. She *take life as it* had to believe in something that would not go away. She had *comes.* to find a security that could not be destroyed or redefined. She found that security in her personal faith. Although life was forever changed and still remained difficult for her, she could now face it because she had chosen a secure place to stand.

Doing life on purpose is not a natural experience. People who live life on purpose don't take life as it comes—they live life with conviction, with passion. Their personal philosophy says they have value, that they are worthy of success.

Each conviction discussed in this book will begin with passionate belief. What you do with each of these life dynamics is significant because you are significant! Acknowledging the need for a chosen personal philosophy will bring you face to face with the spiritual reality of your being. Significance must be something you embrace as the result of belief in yourself as a created and unique individual. Those who do not embrace a belief in God will have a hard time grasping the power of created value.

A personal belief system that insists upon personal perfection is an impossible dream. I personally believe your philosophy must also acknowledge and accept your fallibility. I often hear people talk about the fact that they are dysfunctional and they come from dysfunctional families. I always tell them that although I may not know them personally, I do know one thing about them. We are all dysfunctional, and we all come from dysfunctional families. It is just a matter of degree. We cannot live powerful, purposed lives as long as we are in denial about our fallibility.

PERSPECTIVE: WHAT YOU SEE

The progression continues as your **philosophy** (what you think) creates your **perspective** (what you see). Because of your beliefs, you see life with defined eyes. For the purposed performer, your eyes define life through a powerful sense of purpose. Each day brings with it new possibility. Each challenge is approached positively with the confidence everything ultimately will have an upside. Each day is lived more passionately because of a personal sense of thanksgiving and gratitude.

I have often heard people say "All things work together for good for those who love God." I had a hard time accepting that message in light of so many tragedies I see in life. How could the injustice of abusing the innocent work out for good? How could the destruction and depression of war work out for good? How could the increasing number of homeless people be good? And then, I got in touch with the rest of the story. It is not that all things are good. In fact all things are definitely not good. But seeing the good is a chosen perspective arising out of a personal philosophy of life. It's all in how you choose to look at it.

If your belief system is contingent upon the reflections of the world, then your perspective of life will be inconsistent and depressing. However, if you believe in a powerful, purposed, and positioned existence, you will see each day as having great possibility, no matter what the circumstance or situation.

Positive View

As you adopt the purposed performer attitude, you will see life through positive eyes. Everything will look different to you. I personally regard myself as a positive realist. I don't believe walking around in a state of denial with a smile on my face, pretending everything is great about life, is in any way valuable. I love the way Scott Peck begins his work, *The Road Less Traveled:* "Life is difficult." What an understatement! So the real issue is how you plan to deal with it. You get to choose.

The impact negative people have upon the world around them is amazing to me. I am not talking about people who are courageous and bold enough to question change or who want to present an alternative course for consideration. I'm talking about people who whine and complain about everything. I'm talking about people who can always find someone else to blame for their own inadequacies. I'm talking about people who declare themselves the devil's advocate "for the good of the team."

In my opinion, all negative people should be fired! Barbara, my life partner and business partner, has asked me to temper this statement a bit. So now, in most of my training, I say that all negative people must choose. There is no place for people who want to hold the world hostage with their negative approach to living. Those of you who lead and manage people must come to grips with the energy loss involved in allowing negative people to occupy space on your team. Many of you are paralyzed and afraid to move because you think their productivity outweighs their negativity. Maybe they are key players in your business, or they account for a great deal of revenue. But my experience has shown that if you will remove those negative people, the relief felt by their coworkers will actually result in more productivity. Out of mere gratitude, they will fill in the gap.

People who live life on purpose live with the conviction that life provides positive opportunity every day. I don't mean for you to walk around with a fake smile on your face. In fact, there are times when tears are more appropriate. However, don't take it upon yourself to pull the world down around you. The point is, if you believe right, you have a positive perspective about life, no matter what!

When you look forward to living each day, life takes on new purpose and meaning. It is amazing how many people get up every morning forced to face another day. Many productivity problems in corporate America arise from perspective problems. Those who work in customer service, for instance, have to face difficult people every day. Most don't have a problem with customer service. It is the customers they hate! So often, they dread what they know tomorrow will bring—after all, facing angry customers can be challenging, so say the least. But with that kind of perspective, how impressed will customers be? With proper perspective, those in customer service will give thanks for the problems because they will see them as their reason for being. Difficult people are, in fact, their source for job security.

Passion Shows

A purposed and powerful life philosophy also produces a vision for life filled with passion. Passion is something you cannot hide or pretend. Passion comes from the inside out and is told through your eyes. Passion is a heart issue, arising from a sense of thanksgiving for the opportunity you see before you.

I once got to spend time with one of the most successful residential real estate professionals in North America. I asked her about her business, and it was not long before I was able to see the key to her success. She told me what selling real estate meant to her life. Her husband and her children all played a part in her business. She was so thankful they were able to work side by side every day as a family. At the same time, she loved the prospect of helping people in the midst of making one of the most significant financial investments in their lives—oftentimes an incredible emotional adjustment.

There is no more difficult work in the world than selling houses. There are no more difficult people in the world than those dealing with the tension of moving and financial stress. Yet, here was a person who loved it all. In fact, not long into our conversation, I stopped her and said, "I can see in your eyes the key to your success. Your passion about this business is infectious!" I was not even in the market for a house

It is a matter of allowing your heart to tell your eyes what to see.

and I wanted to buy one from her! What makes the difference? It is clearly a matter of passion developed through a positive perspective. She saw each day as an opportunity to create freedom for herself and for those she loved most. Recognizing each day as a freedom-producing opportunity will create a passion for living that can't be hidden. It is a matter of allowing your heart to tell your eyes what to see.

PERFORMANCE: WHAT YOU DO

Your progression moves from *philosophy* to *perspective* to *performance*. How you live life is simply a reflection of how you see life, which is a result of what you believe about life. Life performance, however, is the bottom line. Any life philosophy that does not result in a powerful, positive, and productive life performance is weak. It amazes me to see people who somehow believe themselves into nonproductive lives. I know people who are so confused about life that they believe it would be better for them not to work and make a living if it means doing jobs they don't feel are worthy of them. Instead of seeing each day as an opportunity to create a course for themselves, they wait on someone to create the course for them. They believe that if it were meant to be, it would be easy to see. But embracing life is seldom easy and requires action.

Life performance is a constantly evolving process. It will take time for your dreams to become reality. First you must see your dream. Your vision for your life serves as a magnet for ultimately living it. Then you can expect the challenges that follow that vision. In fact, experiencing difficulties is essential to enjoying your future success. Positive eyes translate life's difficulties into discovery, learning, and personal growth, rather than discouragement.

Life performance means being productive. Being productive and profitable will be your only security as a professional. While that may sound harsh, it really represents a healthy wake-up call for all of us. There are no free rides. We will not be taken care of because we show up. Tenure is rapidly becoming a debilitating arrangement of the past. Many people spend each day yearning for the right to retire. I think retirement is the greatest and most destructive misconception ever produced by our society. To retire is simply another way of saying, to die. Instead of retiring, we should see each day as an opportunity to graduate to a new and even more challenging level of life. We are all being challenged to grow and develop every day until we die. We may choose to change our course in life but never to quit living. Each day we must be convicted about living life on purpose!

Life performance means living life with conviction. Over the course of the past twenty-five years, I have discovered twelve convictions I believe are essential to purposed living. Each of these convictions, or philosophies, results in a positive perspective that will translate into a purposed performance. I hope you will choose to embrace the philosophy, perspective, and performance progression I will propose in the following chapters. If you get nothing else from this book, however, may you come to realize you do have the power to choose. Consider each of these progressions as potential for your life. They are not inborn. They are developed—they are embraced. Life is a gift. It only makes sense to make the most of it. And living life on purpose is the only choice for those of you who intend to live it abundantly!

Purposed Performance℠
Paradigm

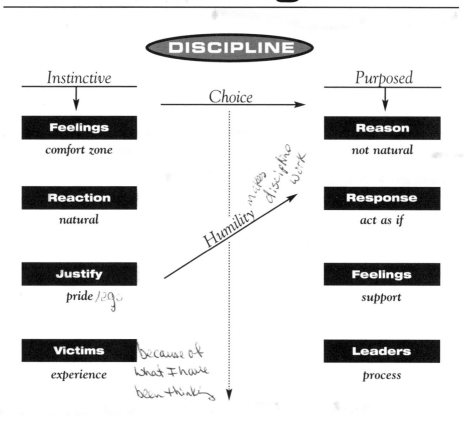

PURPOSED
PERFORMANCE
PARADIGM

Before I can share with you these twelve convictions essential to purposed living, I have to challenge you to make a significant choice in your life. I challenge you to stop living life as a victim! The first conviction I will discuss with you in the next chapter is the *freedom to choose*. Before we get there, though, I have to call upon you to make the most significant choice of your life. In fact, I will draw a line in the sand right here. Throughout history, a line in the sand has confronted people at pivotal moments in their lives. Biblical history tells us of a day when Joshua stood before Israel and drew a line in the sand. He said, "Choose this day whom you will serve. But, for me and my house we will serve Jehovah!" Hundreds of years later, in a little mission called the Alamo, a beleaguered but brave leader named Colonel Travis stood before a group of volunteers and drew a similar line in the sand. He challenged the outnumbered troops to choose to stay and fight for freedom or retreat with dignity. Tough choices! These were choices, however, that changed the course of history. The one I am asking you to make today will change your course of history. It will set you free!

The Purposed Performance Paradigm diagram will be significant to understanding everything I have to say from this point on. So I want to walk you through the thoughts represented by this visual now. Spend some time with these next few pages because I believe the purposed journey beings here.

The **Purposed Performance Paradigm Chart** illustrates that in order to get from how you feel to what you believe, you have to cross the line. In order to get from how you feel to convicted response, you have to cross the line. In order to change your feelings from undependable emotion to supportive encouragement, you have to cross the line.

FEELINGS: OUR COMMON POINT OF BEGINNING

In a very real sense, we are each unique as people. However, we share one powerful reality in common. We are all sensuous beings. In fact, I believe it all begins with how you feel. With every challenge, every choice, and every change we face, our feelings are the first line of engagement. How often have you begun a discussion with the question, "Well, how do you feel about that?" That question in and of itself suggests the challenge we face. How we feel about a given challenge, choice, or change is not the issue. It is, however, the essential point of beginning. What we do with our feelings is the issue!

I believe feelings are our created place of beginning. Having the ability to feel is a blessing we each have been given. Feelings, however, were never meant to lead us. They are too volatile. Contrary to some contemporary songs you might hear or screenplays you might see, feelings cannot be allowed to become your compass for life. If and when that happens, you have begun your victim's journey.

In coaching athletes, and from my own competitive experience, I know feelings *can* greatly impact how you perform. But if you live in the comfort zone of your feelings and allow them to dictate your performance, you will forever be limited. Many times the dividing line between winning and losing comes down to the issue of controlled emotion. Who can keep it together in the heat of the battle? Who loses it when the going gets tough? Who allows the pain of the moment to dictate the effectiveness of the production?

How you feel is not a moral issue—feelings are not a matter of right or wrong. They just are. How you feel is often a product of daily circumstances over which you have no control. I personally deal with the allergy plague. Doctors have told me I'm allergic to about everything I can inhale. While there are those who have health challenges worse than I do, there are days when it doesn't seem possible. On those days, I can really get pitiful. Ask Barbara.

While it's never appropriate to tell another person how they should feel, you can help people deal with their feelings. Fortunately, I have forces around me who help me out of my victim role—people who nudge me back to reality. One of the most significant relationships I have, outside of my relationship to Barbara and my girls, is my friend Michael. For over ten years now, we have worked at keeping each other on track. Michael has called at times when I had given in and gone to bed because I did not feel well. The question he always asks really gets on my nerves, but it also gets to the point. He says, "Will you start feeling better as a result of lying in bed?" He knows the answer, and so do I. No, I will not feel better for having gone to bed. In fact, most of the time I feel worse. For me, a good workout is the best course of action, but it surely doesn't feel like it at the time.

Feelings can play an instinctive lead in your life. Feelings will lead you to get your hands off a hot stove. Your instincts can save you from disaster. Outside of an emergency state, however, feelings have to take another place in your life if you are going to live life on purpose. What do you *do* with how you feel? That is the question.

REACTION: THE NATURAL NEXT STEP

Years ago, someone asked the question of a great teacher, "What is the key to my success?" His answer was unexpected. He said, "Determine the way the majority is going and go the other way." I remember thinking the teacher had surely made an overstatement in order to make a point. After years of working in the field of human performance, however, I have come to the same conclusion. I have found the majority of us, most of the time, react to how we feel.

Never judge the motives of another human being. You never know the path they have just traveled.

Have you ever wanted to take back what you'd just said or done? Of course, we all have reacted to something before we had the time to think it through. It just came out. It was the natural thing to do or say. Stephen Covey tells the story of a train trip home after a long day of working with people. Sitting behind him was a father with children who were out of control. Covey didn't feel like dealing with that kind of frustration after the day he had just had. When he couldn't take it anymore, he turned in his seat and began speaking even before he caught sight of the man and his children, "Could I help you with your children?"

Covey now saw the father had tears streaming down his face as he said, "I wish somebody would. We just buried their mother." For Covey, it was a life-changing moment. Never judge the motives of another human being. You never know the path they have just traveled.

If we allow ourselves to react to how we feel every day, then the day itself will always determine how we are doing. My daughter Jill graduated from college with an undergraduate degree in human communications and business. She plans to pursue her own career and perhaps someday get her MBA. One day she might even join me in my venture. In the meantime, however, she has to put up with me as her father and friend. At times, I will ask her about how her day has been. If she says great, then I usually follow with, why? To which she often says, "Oh, Dad!" She knows what I am trying to do. I want her to see the difference between producing a great day and having a great day happen to you. One is "duplicatable." The other is not.

Unless you allow it, feelings can't control your behavior—it's a choice you make. To say, "I just felt like doing it" doesn't relieve you of responsibility. Too many people try to separate themselves from the responsibility they have for their actions. The parallel life stories of two men clearly illustrate the point I am trying to make. Dave Peltzer is a man with a tragic life story. He is on record as being one of the most abused children in our country's history. Abused by his own mother, he has written a trilogy that chronicles his growing up. The first book is *A Child Called It*, which reflects his earliest memories as a child. It's hard to imagine a child being systematically tortured by one who birthed him, but such was Peltzer's experience. *The Lost Boy* tells of his adolescent years and his final escape from this familial imprisonment. The final book in the trilogy, *A Man Called Dave*, gives us the rest of the story. Peltzer spends his life sharing a message of hope with victims, both of abuse and of life choices. He has chosen to use his inexplicable experience as the catalyst for bringing light to those in darkness.

Another man with a tragic childhood is Charles Manson. His life story has been told in the book *Helter Skelter*. He, too, lived a tragic childhood. Truly the victim of a sad family experience, he, like his mother, spent most of his life in prison. Manson used his tragic experience to bring darkness, pain, and death to the unsuspecting.

You choose the course you take, and you are responsible, no matter how you feel!

Though both had similar childhoods, Manson chose to use his experience to construct a mindset leading to the slaughter of innocent life, whereas Peltzer used his background to help others. Why? What is the difference? The difference is how they chose to react to their life challenges. One chose to bless. The other chose to destroy. Both were choices.

Two teenage boys were responsible for the '99 massacre at Columbine High School near Denver. These two walked in and mowed down their classmates. They may have had inadequate parenting. Their classmates may have cruelly taunted them. There may have been insufficient security. But the truth is, the two boys chose to kill and destroy.

These examples are extreme, but how you feel cannot become your excuse for what you do or for what you do not do. You choose the course you take, and you are responsible, no matter how you feel!

JUSTIFICATION: A HUMAN NEED THAT MUST BE ESTABLISHED

Once you react, you pivot on the brink of truly beginning the victim's journey. It is not too late to turn back. In fact, it is never too late. It just gets much more difficult and much more complicated the further you allow yourself to go in support of your choice. You could stop much of the pain that will surely follow if you will stop right where you are and change your direction.

Unfortunately, at this point, you have two powerful forces working against you. Psychologists might make the case that both forces stem from the same point of origin. For the purpose of our discussion, though, I am going to separate them. The first is the need for internal harmony. The second is pride.

Internal Harmony

Once you have reacted, once your choice has been made, you have an incredible need to justify your actions. Psychologists would call this need cognitive dissonance. You cannot live with the disharmony of actions moving against your belief system. You have to change something. You either reverse your direction and apologize, or you continue on your course and shape your belief system into a filter that will harmonize things for you.

The Arbinger Institute has written an insightful little book entitled *Leadership and Self-Deception*. They would describe this stage in your journey as "entering the box." They identify it as a moment of "self-betrayal." You will go one way or another at this point. That is why this is such a significant moment in your journey. In some ways, you are at the point of no return. While it may be an overstatement, it is really close to how things work. Something else typically happens at this point. Once you have begun the process of justification, you begin to look for others who will agree with you. You need to find people who will agree with the way you think and the choices you make. In the workplace, people of reaction will often look for others of like kind to join them for lunch, for a smoke, or for a drink. Once others enter the picture, it becomes a major act of conviction and courage to change your course. The reason—pride.

Pride

As much as you need harmony within, you need acceptance without almost as much. Once others come into the picture, how you appear before them becomes a force in itself. How many times have you known within your own heart you were on the wrong course, but the public statement you had made or the public position you had taken became a barrier for changing your direction? Maybe you felt like you would lose face. Maybe you would appear to be weak if you were to back down. You could be afraid of the public rejection you might experience. The bottom line is your need to protect your ego. Ego is something we all have and need. It is an essential part of our being. We need to have a healthy sense of pride in ourselves, but when protection of your ego gets in the way of making good choices, then the victim journey is in full swing.

REASON: THE PURPOSED ALTERNATIVE

You do not choose how you feel. It just happens. You do choose, however, what you believe. While feelings cannot and should not ever be denied, you can choose to filter your feelings through the leadership of your reason. What you know and what you believe must be called upon to lead if you ever intend to do life on purpose. The result, whatever it is, will be fueled by your purposed thoughts. You allow your heart to speak from the vantage point of your conviction.

Martin Luther King, Jr., stood in defiance before Washington and all of its power because he believed in a dream. Lincoln stood personally at Gettysburg and spoke even though his advisors objected because he was convicted about the sacrifice made for the cause of freedom. Because Payne Stewart believed in sportsmanship, he did not make Colin Montgomery make a long, last putt in the '99 Ryder's Cup. On and on we could go. If and when you place your feelings into the hands of your personal convictions, then you will be proceeding on a different course.

Obviously, it is difficult to make your feelings bow to the leadership of your knowledge, your beliefs, and your convictions if you have none. But to experience passionate, purposeful living, it is vital for you to continue to work daily to learn and grow. You must come to grips with your belief about life and have your convictions in place. What you know is a product of what you learn and what you experience. What you believe is a product of choices you make about what you know. And your convictions are a product of beliefs forged into fortresses that will stand for you against life's challenges.

RESPONSE: REASON PLACED INTO MOTION

Based upon what you believe, you act. Your beliefs must be strong enough to support the choice you're making. When you move into action, however, you always run the risk of missing it. The people who succeed are the ones who play to win, not just hope not to lose. If you wait to *feel* like it before you do it, you will stay in a perpetual state of paralysis, and that gets you nowhere.

Risk Is the Price You Pay

Michael Jordan has been recognized as the athlete of the twentieth century. Few people in life ever experience the recognition this man has received. What made Jordan great? So many answers could be given. I believe it was because he was willing to put it on the line. He was always the guy with the ball when things got tough. He wanted it that way. As a result, you will always remember Jordan for his last-minute, game-saving shot. The first time Jordan encountered one of those moments, I can assure you, he faced it, not because he felt like it, but because he decided to pay the price.

Risk is the price you pay for extraordinary success. You might remember that as a sophomore Jordan was cut from his high school basketball team. He missed far more shots than he made throughout his incredible career. At times he even looked pretty silly in some public situations. He continued to play, however, in spite of his feelings, and so must you if you ever hope to take control of your life and live it on purpose. You cannot let your feelings control your choices. The positive action you take and positive choices you make cannot always be based upon how you feel in the moment. "Acting as if" must replace "feeling like it" in order to live life on purpose!

Risk is the price you pay for extraordinary success.

FEELINGS: THE SUPPORT WE NEED RETURNS

Feelings were never meant to lead you. They were, however, meant to be your personal support system. When you do what you know you need to do, your feelings are there to say "good for you." When you respond thoughtfully as opposed to reacting emotionally, your feelings will be there to encourage and support your performance.

Earlier, I told about my challenge with allergies and about my friend Michael's way of encouraging me to do what I know helps me most to get going again. How many times have you made yourself go out and do what you needed to do even though you really didn't feel like it? How did you feel when you finished? You are probably like me. You almost always feel better than you would have if you had given into your initial feelings. Your feelings are simply not qualified to lead your life. They are, however, a powerful confirmation of a purposed life response.

CROSS THE LINE

I began this chapter by drawing a line in the sand. Hopefully, you have begun to recognize it by now. The line I have drawn for you is the line of discipline. Here is my definition:

Discipline is a matter of doing what you know you need to do whether you feel like it or not. The rest of this book will be about making disciplined choices. I will present twelve convictions I hope you will add to your system of belief. They will progress from *philosophy* (what you believe), to *perspective* (what you see), to *performance* (what you do). They will never be understood on the victim's side of the line. You will recognize them and be able to embrace them only from the leadership side of the line. You may be like me and move back and forth across the line throughout your life. If you never recognize the need to cross the line, however, you will never take responsibility for your life. I want to challenge you to cross the line and choose to live life on purpose. If you are ready and willing to make the journey, then proceed. Choosing not to live life on purpose is choosing to live life as a victim. I cannot believe you would ever really choose to be a victim, would you? Think about it. Get ready, and let's begin the journey you were born to take.

FREEDOM
TO CHOOSE

Have you ever stopped to think about just how many choices you have to make every day? By the end of most days, you really don't want to make one more decision. One of the biggest frustrations Barbara and I have faced in our marriage lies in choosing a restaurant for the evening. I usually begin by asking "Where do you want to go?" She then will follow with "I don't care, where do you want to go?" Which results in my response which is usually "I don't care, where do you want to go?" To which she will say more creatively, "It really doesn't make any difference to me, you choose." Can you relate? The point is that having the freedom to choose in life brings its own brand of challenge.

Freedom is a precious commodity to us Americans. Countless people have died for the cause. Yet, the most significant freedom in life is one that you might not yet have claimed. It is free, and it's life's most meaningful gift: You have the freedom to choose. Living life on purpose begins with conviction about your freedom to *choose*. Unfortunately, it is a choice most people will never make because of the consequences involved.

There are times as adults when we really wish Mom and Dad were there to choose for us. For several years I worked on a university campus, and I loved to hear students complaining about the number of decisions they had to face every day. Some would talk to me about how they looked forward to graduation so there wouldn't be as many decisions to make. Unfortunately, I had to help them see that life is about making choices. We never graduate beyond the point of needing to choose.

Because making choices every day is not always easy, many people try to opt out of the responsibility. For the most part, the empowerment movement in corporate America has not worked because most working people would rather not accept the responsibility that goes along with making decisions. They would rather someone else choose for them because then they would not be responsible for the outcome. As a result, there is a growing imbalance in compensation in most organizations because compensation is directly related to a person's willingness to accept risk. Simply put, those who are willing to risk more, make more.

Not wanting to be responsible for choices comes out of insecurity, which can come in various forms. For some, it is the risk of failing. They say not trying at all is better than trying and failing. Unfortunately, some management mentalities in corporate America serve to inspire this particular fear. I heard one chief executive of an organization say proudly that his people know if they choose a course he has not laid out for them, and it doesn't work, they are fired. If they will do as they are told, they will not be held responsible. And corporate America wonders why productivity is such a problem.

Others fear choosing because it means change, and change will launch them into the world of the unknown. For them, knowing what is going to happen, even if it is not healthy, is better than choosing a journey into the unknown. I have spent a lot of time working with women who are victims of abuse. It is amazing how many women will escape near-death experience only to return for more after things have calmed down. Some would say they go back because they believe it is what they deserve. Others say that it has to do with what they think they are worth. Or maybe it's because they grew up in a home where they saw it happen to their mothers and so they believe it is their destiny. No doubt, there is insight found in all of those explanations. I believe the greater issue, however, lies in the challenge of making responsible choices. Choosing to make a life change is never easy. It's just easier to let someone else make the decision, even if the decision results in abuse. To choose freedom is to choose responsibility. Freedom without responsibility is simply bondage in disguise.

> *Freedom without responsibility is simply bondage in disguise.*

Taking responsibility for your choices is essential to doing life on purpose. If you are not willing to accept the challenge of choosing, you will continue to live life as a victim. If, however, you are ready to take responsibility for your life, you are ready to begin. It all begins with you and what you choose. Each choice kicks off a series of events that will determine your progression in life.

PHILOSOPHY: POWER AND FREEDOM

Life brings new challenges every day. You rarely have control over what those challenges will be or when they will come. If you ever want to experience the liberating power of choosing, you must first embrace this fact: While we rarely have control of what happens to us, we always have the power to choose how we will respond. This particular truth is central to any hope of living life on purpose, and one any person can embrace, no matter what the circumstance.

The most significant personal choice I had to make as a young man came in ninth grade. I decided to quit playing football and start playing tennis. To fully appreciate the magnitude of my choice you would have to understand what football meant to boys in Texas in the '60s. You would also have to know that I was put on notice early in my life that if I planned to go to college it would be by means of a scholarship. I started playing football when I was six years old. Groomed to be a quarterback, I met high school coaches before I got into junior high, and they encouraged me to keep throwing that ball. I was expected to continue to grow and ultimately move right into high school and beyond on the wings of football. Football would be my pass into college. Things stayed pretty much on course until the eighth grade. Who could have expected that everyone else would grow, and that I would not? It became obvious to me that my future in this game would be limited if I didn't have size. And I couldn't even see over the line!

I picked up a tennis racquet in the summer before my ninth grade, and it was an immediate love affair. While I was encouraged to know that athletics could still be my ticket to college, I unfortunately had football coaches who did not appreciate my reasoning.

Tennis was not fully recognized as a "man's" sport at that stage in the game in Texas. Coaches expected me to hang in there and wait for the physical growth they knew would come—and stay committed to the team. Sleepless nights and needless persecution couldn't dissuade me. I was determined to get to college, and I knew that tennis would be my best bet. When I signed a full scholarship at the end of my senior year, I couldn't wait to find my football coaches. No one in my class signed a football scholarship that year. Thankfully, I grew more than six inches by the time I left college, but I'm glad I didn't base my future on it.

The point of this personal story is to let you know that the need to exercise the power to choose is something that we encounter early in life. And I'm thankful for parents and people who supported me in making this tough decision.

The Library of Congress publishes a list of the world's most influential books, and one book in particular seems to always make their list. The book is *Man's Search for Meaning* by Viktor Frankl. I remember the impact the book had on my life the first time that I read it. Viktor Frankl was a Jewish psychiatrist who lived in the wrong place at the wrong time. A victim of the atrocities of Nazi Germany, he watched his wife and family tortured and killed in gas chambers. He lived through the horrors of the worst Nazi camps and yet survived. Frankl believed that while he had no choice over his imprisonment physically, he did have the power to choose how he would respond. He chose not to be a prisoner. While they could control him physically, they couldn't control his mind. They couldn't imprison his heart. Upon liberation, interviewed prison guards confessed that, in relationship to Frankl, they knew they were more the prisoner than he was. In spite of overwhelming physical conditions, Frankl not only survived, he thrived. He was free even while in prison because he believed in his power to choose.

Helen Keller, Franklin Roosevelt, Martin Luther King, Jr., Gandhi, Nelson Mandela, Mother Teresa, the list could go on and on. The most influential and inspiring people who have ever lived embraced this philosophy of choice. They all had in common the belief that no matter what obstacle they might face, no one could take from them their power to choose. And this power provided freedom both for them and those they served.

Perspective: Possibility and Opportunity

Years ago, in the second chapter of my professional career, I worked for one of the world's largest manufacturer of hospital-related products. It was my first run at selling tangible products. We were challenged as a sales team to promote certain products, one of which was a large and rather expensive piece of equipment. Success in our annual sales competition was contingent upon selling our quota of this equipment. When my regional manager called to check on my progress, I told him that I had really struck out. No one was interested. In fact, they wouldn't even let me in to seriously discuss it. He asked me about one large hospital in my territory, and I told him I had tried with them and failed. They weren't interested. He told me he would pick me up the next day and we would make a call on that hospital together. I tried to stop him by explaining again that they were not interested. I had tried—they wouldn't let me in. None of that dissuaded him. So, the next morning he picked me up and we went on the sales call together. Now to understand the full impact of what I experienced, you have to know a little bit about this regional manager. He was a Silver Star winner in Viet Nam, and he translated his war experience into everything that he did. He'd faced enemies who were determined to kill him. He'd been faced with the challenge of taking over enemy territory. So he had a little different perspective about this hospital challenge of mine. When we arrived at the hospital, I tried to open my door to get out and he stopped me. He said we were not ready yet. He told me to sit back and relax. He did the same. He then reached forward and pushed a cassette tape into the player. Pulsating music began playing. As this instrumental piece with a military flare to it played and picked up momentum, he began to pulsate with the music. I thought he had lost his mind. At a climactic moment, he looked at me and said, "Now we are ready!" He kicked the door open and headed for the hospital. I followed along behind. Within two hours, he managed to gain audience with every major decision maker in the place. Before he was through, we left with a purchase order for two pieces of equipment. I couldn't believe it! This was the same place that had shut me out. What was the difference? This sales manager of mine saw things differently because he had a belief system that was different. He believed he had control over how he responded in any situation and that with the right approach success would be his.

What you believe greatly influences your approach to life. It dictates how you see life around you. Great athletes are great because they look at things differently. Yes, Michael Jordan made shots that pulled victory out of the jaws of defeat. And he will forever be known for his clutch shooting and his ability to perform in pressure-packed situations. He saw pressure as opportunity, and when the game was on the line, Jordan wanted the ball. He believed that he couldn't enjoy victory to its fullest unless he was willing to risk defeat. He was secure in the fact that losing was a big part of winning. He played to win as opposed to just playing not to lose.

If you believe you always have the power to choose then life offers new possibility every day.

You see what you believe. If you believe you always have the power to choose then life offers new possibility every day. The freedom and power you gain provide opportunity for you, no matter what the situation. I know that may be too much to swallow. You might wonder what Viktor Frankl gained from his concentration camp experience. The truth is, Frankl gained immeasurably from his experience. In fact, in many ways he was in the right place at the right time. He left the horrors of Nazi Germany a more powerful man than ever before. He gained insight that changed the quality of life for many people. It didn't come, however, without a price: He lost his family; he was left alone. In reality, that was the part over which he had no control. He could not have saved his family. He could not control Hitler or his henchmen. He could control only his heart and mind. He could control only what he saw. And, as a result, when he saw those German guards he saw the real prisoners. He saw the misery of his fellow prisoners as opportunity to provide care. He came out of it all with a perspective that forever changed the world of psychology. Without the pain, he would never have known the power.

Without the pain, he would never have known the power.

Recently, I met a woman who has been through the tragedy of midlife divorce. Experiencing pain and disappointment she never thought possible, she spent months dealing with the grief and loss. On her road to recovery, however, she found opportunity. She found herself in a position to help women who were experiencing the same kind of trauma. She effectively helped others and, in the process, she benefited the most. She chose to see possibility in her conflict and opportunity in her loss.

At times we will make perspective choices that alter the way we believe. Chances are good that this woman did not at first believe there was any value in her divorce. While she had no control over it, she learned that even in the horrors of her personal tragedy opportunity would come. She now faces life with an entirely new sense of power and freedom. She sees possibility in every day and every situation. She has new sparkle and energy in her eyes. She is now living life on purpose.

PERFORMANCE: CONFIDENT AND POSITIVE

When your beliefs are liberating and powerful, your vision will be clear. Each day will provide possibility that others only wish they could experience. Opportunity can be seen in any and every situation, and learning becomes your way of life. As a result, your life performance takes on a new look. You can face each day with the confidence of knowing you are going to succeed no matter what. You can face each day with a perspective that is positive and productive. And you will be just the kind of person this world needs.

I believe that all negative people need to be fired immediately. I know that I have already said that, but I want to make sure that you get it. I've also tried to soften that just a little by suggesting that negative people need to choose. But the presence of whining, complaining, blaming people is so destructive that you can't wait long to make the call. They suck the life out of any organization. At the very least, they need to be challenged to make their choice, today! The tragedy is, too many people go to work every day with a negative perspective. They dread the challenges of the day. They have no confidence in their ability to perform—they're afraid of the very things they have to do every day. No wonder morale is such a problem for most organizations.

When you are able to see every day as opportunity, life becomes a more positive experience. You don't have to be in denial to be positive, but you must believe in your power and ability to respond to life when it happens to you. With that kind of security, it is possible to be positive and confident in any and every situation. Someone might ask how skills and preparation fit into the equation. Later in the book, we'll talk about the dynamic role these two factors play in our lives. But, foundationally speaking, it is possible to be confident even in the face of situations where we are ill prepared and uninformed. However, we must be able to see every situation as a learning opportunity. We must be okay with our ability to make mistakes. Even when we have to admit our failure in a given moment, we can be positive because we know we will learn a valuable lesson.

Interestingly enough, that kind of honesty will also produce powerful relationships, but that is another conviction altogether.

Productive energy radiates from people who see life through positive eyes.

Productive energy radiates from people who see life through positive eyes. We enjoy being around positive people. They attract like magnets. It is amazing to see the difference that attitude and perspective make in the presence of a person. People who have been negative and insecure can become positive and confident when they make the choice to change. Living life on purpose is an inside-out story.

Change is a much-discussed phenomenon in our world today. It is almost as if we think it is a new concept, but actually, change is a natural and normal part of our lives. Look in the mirror. You change a little every day. The difference is that natural change doesn't require choice. It will happen whether you like it or not. Positive change, however, requires choice. You can choose to accept natural change or you can choose to fight it. The choice is yours. Life's outcome depends upon your ability to embrace change. No matter how you've approached life in the past, you can change tomorrow.

CHOOSING TO LIVE LIFE ON PURPOSE

The power to choose is yours. The responsibility for your choices is yours. You have no one else to blame for the way you choose to respond to life. It is your deal. When you embrace this God-given power, then you will come to know freedom. Liberation from the fear of the unknown in life will be yours, and you will be secure in your power to choose.

Choosing is an action word. It means you are going to do things differently. But for that to happen, something essential must take place: The way you talk to yourself must change. In most cases, you are your own worst enemy. If others said to you the things you say to yourself, you wouldn't choose to be around them long. You, however, are stuck with you. The good news is, you have control over the things you say to yourself. You may not be able to change and control others, but you can change yourself.

TAKE THE CHALLENGE

From this point on, at the end of each chapter, you will be introduced to a series of affirmations. These are positive thoughts you should tell yourself. Read them and repeat them. We are going to accumulate a great list of positive thoughts before this book is over. This chapter, however, is where we can begin. Choose to think differently. Choose to see life differently. Choose to embrace life every day with a spirit of optimism and anticipation!

AFFIRMATIONS

I believe in my power to choose.
I believe in my freedom to choose.
I see possibility in every day of my life.
I see opportunity to learn in every situation.
I am positive about life no matter what.
I am confident in my power to perform.

THE POWER
OF PEOPLE

One thing you can depend upon every day is the presence of people in your life. Like them or not, they're there. It is a regular part of my life to finish a day of work with people and then have to catch a flight to another city or to return home. The last thing I feel like doing is to sit next to a person on the plane who wants to talk. In fact, if there were a "No Talking Section" available, I'd probably be there. It's good there's no such thing though because the most insightful moments I've ever spent have been with people in flight who have incredible stories to tell. Although some of their stories are more interesting than others, they all have them. Many of the stories I have heard I have been able to use in my work. In reality, the people who come into my world are the source for all that I have come to know and love about people. Until you recognize the significance that the people around you play, you'll never live life purposefully.

Customer service has become the mantra in the business world. Every company is involved in some dimension of customer service. The service might be to external customers who are investing in you and the service you offer. Or it might be to internal customers you interface with every day. One way or another, you need people in order to be the success you hope to be. Don't you hate it? I have heard people say that if they didn't have to deal with people, customer service would be easy. But the truth is, if it weren't for the troubled people around you, you probably wouldn't have a job. Troubled people looking for help fuel job opportunity for the world.

Troubled people looking for help fuel job opportunity for the world.

I'm getting ahead of myself some. The real question is, How do you feel about the people in your world? Do you wake up every day excited about the opportunity you will have to live and work and love and play with others? Most people wake up every day living among family. It is a blessing for most; it's a desire for everyone. Unfortunately, there are those who don't see family and people close to them as a blessing, but as objects of utility. They see them as frustrations that have to be tolerated. They see them and treat them as though they are expendable. Intention is not the issue. The real issue lies in how you deal with their presence in your life.

For years, I have counseled and coached men and women who are trying to make their marriages work. Many times they seek help before it is too late. Other times, unfortunately, they've waited too long; the damage has been done. Time, inconsiderate treatment, sometimes abuse has served to create a chasm they can never cross. Interestingly enough, women tend to be the ones who come seeking change before it is too late. I typically will ask them to identify their major frustration. The number-one answer by far is that they can't get their husbands to talk to them. Through tears they explain how their husbands won't communicate in any meaningful way. I always love their response when I ask them how well their husbands communicated with them before they got married. Nine out of ten times, they will look down and reflect that communication had never been a real part of their relationship. For you not yet married: Any challenge you face before marriage will only be magnified once you are married. Getting married will not fix problems; it will only intensify them.

Men, on the other hand, are different. They don't get too emotionally involved at the request of their wives. They play it pretty cool and maintain their innocence. They point to her as the problem. The scene is dramatically different, however, when the husband comes in before his wife, because typically she has already left him—many times with someone who has communicated meaningfully with her in the emotional absence of her husband. The change is amazing. I have seen grown men cry and shake uncontrollably. They can't believe she is gone. They plead and pray for one more chance. Too often the chance never comes. Too much damage has been done.

People cannot be taken for granted. They play a dramatic role in our lives, and we need them. Why is it that many, if not most times, we don't recognize it until they are gone? But the frustration in their presence can't compare with the pain of their absence. Years ago, I attended a funeral that I will never forget for a woman in her eighties whom I really didn't know well. She was a faithful member of a local church, and it obviously meant a lot to her. At the funeral, I have never seen publicly expressed grief like I witnessed with her children. They sobbed. They moaned. They fell upon the casket. They couldn't let her go. Her grandson shared with me an insight that is too often the case: These same children who now grieved so dramatically were the same children who had no time for their mother when she was alive. She lived a lonely life. Neighbors and church friends became her family. Her kids were dealing with the consequence of taking a person for granted.

People cannot be taken for granted.

Grief for a loved one can happen in any of our lives. It can even be for children who grow up too soon. My three girls are all grown now, but it seems only yesterday that they were my little girls. Now life has changed. In many ways, they are gone. Sometimes it happens that we lose friends and loved ones to death before we are ready. I dislike the way we categorize people once they are diagnosed with cancer or some other seemingly incurable disease. We say that they are terminal. We somehow believe that the disease produced that reality. Disease never makes us terminal. We are all terminal by our very nature. Life is brief for us all, and we simply cannot afford to take the people in our lives for granted.

The moments we have with them are too special to waste.

Purposed living recognizes the power of people in our lives. We cannot live meaningful and healthy lives without them. We can't really even get a true reflection of ourselves without reflection from the people in our world. Family, friends, coworkers, customers, neighbors, visitors all impact our lives. We either purpose their impact or we will be victimized by their impact. Purposed living passionately embraces people. Think about moving forward and choosing this progression.

PHILOSOPHY: PRIVILEGE AND RESPECT

The people who live around me every day are the unique product of divine workmanship. They have the special imprint of God. They each are gifted in their own way. It is a privilege to live in this kind of powerful production. They deserve my respect because of who and whose they are. Who am I to judge, disrespect, condemn, or mistreat someone with those kinds of credentials?

Because I travel a great deal, I have the opportunity to see people interaction at its most intense level. The airports of the world provide a great laboratory for studying people. It is appalling to me how often I see people disrespect and abuse others. I think many of the agents who stand at the airport ticket counters have a special place reserved in heaven. I once watched as a man in a very expensive suit with a very impressive set of luggage threw an absolute fit at a ticket coun-ter. He was verbally abusive to the agent, and then he picked up the poles used to guide passengers to the counter and launched them across the room. It was incredible. He obviously didn't stop to think about what that agent might do to him.

I heard someone tell for truth a similar story: A man loudly cursed the agent as he stomped away to catch his flight. My friend stepped up to the counter and immediately commended the agent for the calm way in which he had handled the situation. The agent appreciated the compliment but said he really didn't deserve it. He said that he was able to keep his cool because he knew something the man did not know. While he was on his way to New York, his baggage was on its way to Mexico. What goes around too often does come around.

Seeking to control others is probably the most prevalent failing among human beings, and it is also the most disrespectful.

What would cause one person to tee off like that on another? No doubt, the man was being driven by some kind of personal fear. Beyond that, however, he obviously regarded others around him as a means to his end. He saw them as being purposed to serve him. As a result, it was natural for him to lash out and abuse a person he could not control. Seeking to control others is probably the most prevalent failing among human beings, and it is also the most disrespectful. Couples fall in love and get married because they love each other just the way they are. Then they almost immediately set out to change each other into their own image. However, if they had been that way in the first place, they never would have married them to begin with. Somehow, we see ourselves as being qualified to determine how other people are supposed to be.

Families provide a great laboratory for seeing "the control game" in action. That would be particularly true in my family and with me specifically. Barbara and I have been married over thirty years and have been blessed with three beautiful daughters and now two grandchildren. In many ways, the success of our family is a tribute to Barbara and the perseverance of our daughters Angela, Jill, and Meredith. Because I was raised in a home with all boys, I had a hard time adjusting to my role as father to three delicate daughters. I really saw myself as their protector, which is another way of saying that I saw myself as the one who was called upon to control their lives. Angela, my oldest, had the misfortune of having to raise me as a father. She is a bright, talented, and strong-willed young woman who did not want my controlling presence in her life. As a result, we fought many "power wars," particularly in her teenage years. I wouldn't allow her to make her own choices and deal with her own consequences, making her adolescent years much more difficult than they needed to be. Fortunately, she has loved me through my insanity, and we have an extremely close relationship.

The experience with Angela changed the way I faced my role as father to Jill and Meredith. Instead of trying to control them, I gave them room to make their mistakes. It was hard to watch them as they had to deal with life's consequences, but I know they are who they are today because of the lessons they learned. During both Jill's and Meredith's senior years in high school, we removed all traditional constraints from their lives. They had no real curfews. Beyond being a positive part of the family and obeying the law, they were on their own. It was quite a departure from my original paradigm, but I knew it was best for them. They were allowed to make their choices and deal with their consequences while we were still there to love them. In working with freshmen on a university campus for a number of years, I watched many of them struggle and suffer because they had never been allowed to choose for themselves while at home. I am convinced that the control we try to heap on our children is many times more for our protection than it is for theirs. In fact, I believe that our effort to control others rises out of a deeper desire to protect ourselves. We must admit that the best interest of others is not always our primary motivation.

Seeing people as the product of divine workmanship brings a new sense of relationship into view.

Seeing people as the product of divine workmanship brings a new sense of relationship into view. In reality, we are privileged to have our life partners. We are not placed with them to change them or control them, but rather to appreciate and celebrate them. Because of their divine heritage, they deserve our respect as opposed to our ridicule. People are purposed in this life. As people, we share a journey; we don't have to walk it alone. People are all around us with the same needs and the same fears we face. We need each other! By believing in the powerful privilege and purpose of people, life takes on entirely new meaning and possibility.

PERSPECTIVE: **PURPOSE AND POTENTIAL**

With a sense of privilege in your heart and with respect as your response, people take on a new appearance in your life. Instead of seeing them as necessary evils, they become potentially powerful life partners. All of your relationships in life will suddenly come alive with meaning and purpose. Your desire for positive relationships will become your life theme.

Think about the relationships in your life. Begin with your family. Parents are hard to understand because many times as children we believe they are confused. Having become a parent myself now, I have an entirely new appreciation for what my own parents went through. My father worked hard all of his life to provide for his family. His parenting skills were limited to say the least. He expressed his love through his commitment and hard work. He supported me in the only way he knew how. He never missed a game that I played. I still remember how he helped me move into my dorm as a freshmen in college. He was proud of me because I had received a full scholarship as an athlete. My room was on the third floor, and we made trip after trip up those stairs. My dad was not in good shape physically; in fact, he was in horrible shape. But he trudged tirelessly up those stairs again and again with sweat dripping off of his face. I will always remember that experience as a living expression of my father's love.

My mother is a selfless servant. She was, and is, committed to her children. I remember the way she patiently calmed my fears when I first had to deal with the dark. She woke up at 4:00 A.M. to help me throw my paper route. She was always there with a word of encouragement. She was there to wipe my brow with a cool rag when I had high fever. She always believed in me even when I didn't believe in myself. Parents are positioned by God to partner with us in our growth process. They are his gift to us.

It is in marriage that we see ourselves most clearly. Through this partnering relationship we discover the true meaning of intimacy. Someone has said that intimacy is being able to share our most present fear with complete confidence.

Barbara knows me better than any person in the world. She knows the good, the bad, and the ugly. With her, I have no place to hide. Through her, I have learned the true meaning of love. She's my best friend—she loves me in spite of me. I have given her so many reasons to let go, but she loves me anyway. Barbara has given me a glimpse of God's love.

Children are another incredible relationship blessing in life. In fact, they probably provide the greatest seminar of all. About the time you think you know something, your children will help you know otherwise. Our three daughters have defined our lives for the past twenty-eight years. The interesting thing about having multiple children is to see how unique they each are. I have already confessed to my ineptness in dealing with the adolescent challenges of our oldest daughter. Angela came out of the womb believing she knew best. One of her earliest prayers was for God to help her believe that Mom and Dad knew best when she knew that she did. Through her challenges as an adolescent, my concept of fatherhood changed. I learned that my children were, in truth, not my children at all but God's, and we just get to share them with him for a while. He doesn't want me to play the role of keeper. Rather, he wants me to be there to love and encourage them in their choices. Angela taught me more than any book ever could. She is my daughter and she has grown to be a special friend.

My daughter Jill is a unique young woman. She is the original strong-willed child. She was determined to create her own course from the very beginning. Jill is intense. In many ways, she has provided me a glimpse of many of my own tendencies. She sees things the way they ought to be, and it becomes her mission to get it right. She has very little patience with herself and sometimes with others. At the same time, her drive makes her a leader in every sense of the word. I have watched her mature into an incredible young woman. She is learning to blend her intensity for life with an enjoyment of life. She is teaching me how to live. She is my daughter and she is a special friend.

Meredith is something special. She walks to the beat of a different drummer. She always has. I sometimes say that she is loosely tethered to this earth. She is a happy person with a beautiful smile. She loves people and they love her. She is patient, faithful, and longsuffering with her friends. As a result, she has many. She has her own idea about clothes. I have always enjoyed buying clothes for the women in my family, but I have never been able to get a clear grasp on her style. Her fashion page, however, is clear in her mind. Meredith is teaching me the joy of living. She is showing me that it is important to follow your dreams. She is my daughter and she is my special friend.

I have been blessed with a father- and mother-in-law who have shown me joy in living. I have had teachers and coaches who have allowed me to see the value of being committed to the growth and the development of others. I have friends who show me the strength that comes from having the support of significant others in your life. The list could go on and on. People have been placed in my life for a special purpose. And they have been placed in yours for that same reason. They are a gift from the One who knows just what you need—they are purposed in our lives. We are privileged to have them in our lives. We have greater potential because they are there. If you see people through those eyes, then the world around you will take on a new, fresh, and exciting look.

PERFORMANCE: PARTNERSHIP AND PRIVILEGE

We live a shared experience. The people around us are not meant to be objects for our consumption. Rather, they are our partners traveling with us from this world to the next. Each day I have the opportunity to join hands with the people around me to make this journey more meaningful. By partnering with my life companions, I gain the potential for a powerful life performance that is impossible for those who exist in a "solo," delusional mindset.

It is impossible to avoid the people around you. It is also complete denial to pretend you have no impact upon your world. Whether you want to be or not, you are a leader in your world. Leadership is ultimately a matter of influence, and you have it. We all do. It's just a matter of how we choose to use the privilege.

Focus

Specifically to remind me that accomplishing my life goals will come through the combined efforts of life partners, some of whom I have yet to meet, I decided to name our company The Tappe Group. Barbara is my legal partner in this venture, but her contribution goes far beyond what is written into the corporate structure. Without her, I would not be able to concentrate on the things that require my attention. In fact, I believe partnering with others allows us to focus on the things that we do best. A little book by Donald O. Clifton and Paula Nelson entitled *Soar with Your Strengths* provides excellent insight into the value of staying focused upon the things that are your strengths. I couldn't be in business if it weren't for the partners I meet every day who make my life possible. At this very moment, I am in flight from Dallas–Ft. Worth to Albuquerque. I promise you, this would not be possible without the cooperative efforts of the good people of American Airlines.

New Strengths

I also believe that partnering with others provides needed strengths that I don't have. I have had an alliance of heart and mind with the Blanchard–Schaefer organization, an outstanding creative marketing, public relations, and advertising organization. Creative statements I have made about my company from the beginning have been carefully shaped through their leadership. They have provided a communicative touch and direction that I would not have had without them.

Accountability

I mentioned earlier my unique friendship with Michael Brooks. Mike and I have so much in common. We are close to the same age, although he is older, a fact he reminds me of regularly. We both have been blessed and humbled by three bright daughters. We both also married above us. For years, Mike and I have enjoyed a very determined accountability relationship. Each year we spend several days preparing and sharing our life plan for the coming year. We talk to each other no less than once a week for the expressed purpose of staying on track. I know that without this relationship of encouragement and accountability, I would never have grown through many of the life challenges I have faced.

Only by purposefully weaving accountability into your life will you ever hope to do those things you simply do not feel like doing. Presently, I enjoy that kind of relationship with Dr. Victor Avis in Staten Island, New York. Vic is both a client and a friend. Last year we recognized together our mutual need for more physical fitness. So we both have committed to aerobic exercise three times per week, each and every week. For each time we do not exercise in a week, we must pay the other person $100. It could cost me up to $300 each week if I were to choose not to make it happen. Now, ask me if I have missed even once over the past year and a half. Are you kidding? I actually did come close one week. I got out of town without my running gear and I needed to pick up one more time for the week. So, I went to the sporting goods store and bought $175 worth of shorts and shoes. When I told Vic, he said that I could have saved money by just sending him the $100. Vic's wife, Kim, has told me that Vic has run when he was sick. And he has run more than once a day to keep his commitment. What is that all about? Think about it. Don't you get more committed the moment you say to another person that you will be some-place or that you will do something? Here is the rule: Public commitment made by choice to someone will always provide the positive personal tension necessary to keeping it.

Only by purposefully weaving accountability into your life will you ever hope to do those things you simply do not feel like doing.

Accountability in corporate America is a much-misunderstood relationship. For most people, it is a negative concept. It signals confrontation and control. To the contrary, accountability is the most positive force you can bring into your life and into the life of your organization. It can also be the most powerful. Being accountable provides you reason to celebrate. Once you get clear about what you want to accomplish and are actively committed to getting it accomplished, the games begin. Watching and applauding your progress becomes an important part of the growth process. That is why, on a personal basis, so many are investing in trainers in order to help them achieve some of the physical goals that have been so elusive for them. My wife, Barbara, can personally testify to the power of that kind of accountability. For over two years, she has worked with a personal trainer at the gym three times per week. She would quickly tell you that because of both her financial obligation and her personal integrity for keeping the commitment both to herself and to another person, rarely has Barbara missed her training time.

We all have the power to choose to be accountable.

Accountability in the workplace must become the personal choice and desire of the American workforce if we ever hope to meet the performance challenges of the twenty-first century. Performance reviews must become more than annual moments of confrontation and disappointment over compensation. They must become times of celebration and performance clarification! Instead of being annual moments to dread, they must become regular moments of recognition. While their involvement and cooperation is obviously important, the responsibility for creating this relationship does not belong primarily to the manager. It is only, however, when an employee begins to see and seek accountability as a professional growth tool that powerful things begin to happen. We all have the power to choose to be accountable. We have no one to blame but ourselves when we are not.

PEOPLE MAKE POWERFUL PARTNERS

People are all around us. They make a major difference in our lives, and if we choose, that difference can be positive. They are presently doing more for us than we typically recognize or appreciate. In fact, *we* are typically more significant to the people around us than we recognize or appreciate. Because of the significant partners in our lives, we are able to stay focused on what we do well. Because of willing people in our lives, we are able to make ourselves accountable to reaching higher than we ever could on our own. Because of relationships with people we are able to experience encouragement, to have company in dealing with and learning from the challenges of life.

As I am writing these words, I received a telephone call from a person who is both a client and a friend. We talked some about a new business venture in which he is involved. It was exciting for me to be able to hear about his personal growth and new challenge. It was also a joy to be able to offer my support and help. Beyond business, we also talked about family and about a personal loss he is presently experiencing because of cancer. Having been through that same kind of loss, I was able to offer some words of encouragement. Relationships are the most powerful gift we can have in this life. Remember, relationships are only possible because people are reality. Celebrate the people in your life!

TAKE THE CHALLENGE

Identify three relationships you have in your life and think about the difference they have made and are making in your life. Begin a new relationship with yourself through journaling. Remember, this is for you. Don't try to impress anyone with your literary prowess. Just discover again the power of people in your life. Discover for yourself the difference they are making in your life and the contribution you are making in theirs. Once the picture is before you, you will be better able to make necessary life adjustments.

AFFIRMATIONS

I see people as a powerful force in my life.
I am thankful for the people in my life.
I respect the people in my life.
I appreciate and applaud the strengths of others.
I am who I am because of what others help me to be.
I look for the opportunity to help others.

THE HEART
OF MOTIVATION

Dorothy is one of my heroes. I only knew her for a few years, yet she left a lasting impression on my life. For thirty-five years she taught and challenged children. She "adopted" them all; they were "her kids." No matter who you were or what role you played, you didn't want to mess with one of Dorothy's kids. During the time I spent with her, I watched her fight courageously against the ravages of cancer. She had been fighting the fight for years when I came into her life. She taught me so much about living and dying; however, there is one picture of her I will never forget.

During the last week of her life I came into her room and found her with one of her kids. The young girl was sitting on the edge of her bed holding Dorothy's hand. The girl's mother related to me how Dorothy had served to change her daughter's life. She helped her believe in herself. Through indescribable pain, Dorothy continued to praise this girl. She hugged her and placed her on center stage. She was her teacher to the very end. She was not being driven by a salary or job description. She was being driven by a force deep within. All of her kids felt it. Dorothy was their hero.

Motivation is not just *an* issue. It is *the* issue. Motivation is a powerful and a personal issue. Most people go through life waiting for something or someone to motivate them. But it just doesn't work that way. And if it does, the result will always be short-lived. So ask yourself, Do I produce enough personal fuel to energize myself as a person?

Extrinsic motivation is the kind of pep-rally experience we have all come to know and love. I remember those great moments during my Texas school years when everyone would gather in the school gym for a pep rally before football games. The band would be rockin' and the cheerleaders would be jumpin' and the coach would be predicting victory. The team was pumped! We were winners! Then came the kick-off.

In my short football career, among other things, I returned kick-offs. I remember those moments when the ball would be in my hands, and I would look up only to see the other team bearing down upon me. Of course, my team would all be down. We weren't very good, which might give you another insight into why I ultimately took up tennis. I remember wondering where the band was now! Where were those cheerleaders? Where was that coach? Pep rallies were fun, but when it came down to it, they had very little "in the moment" value. Don't get me wrong. Even today pep rallies are fun, and they have their place. Attending a great motivational seminar produces a terrific emotional high. Unfortunately, you have to return that voicemail when you get back to the office. How many times has that emotional high been extinguished within a few moments of returning to the field of battle?

The motivation I am talking about will withstand those challenging moments. In fact, the motivation we will discuss in this chapter is not contingent upon life that is happening around you. Rather, it is fueled by conviction that is being produced within you.

Intrinsic motivation feeds conviction you carry deep in your soul. It is the kind of power that has produced heroes like Gandhi, Martin Luther King, Jr., Nelson Mandela, and Mother Teresa. It has also produced visionaries like Walt Disney, Charles Schultz, and Bill Gates. It has been the driving force behind great athletes like Jim Thorpe, Jackie Robinson, and Arnold Palmer. More importantly, it has produced and it continues to produce powerful stories through the lives of parents, children, teachers, entrepreneurs, salesmen, and managers. What makes some people go and others stop—or even worse never start?

In my experience, as both a life performer and a life coach, it all comes back to the power of a person's *why*. How strong is your *why*? Before tackling any challenge, it is the question you must ask yourself. If you are a person trying to help others face life challenges or make life choices, you need to get them in touch with their reason why. If their why is not strong enough, they will not do what it takes when the going gets tough.

Here is a paradox for you to consider: When you get clear about the need for getting something done, don't you typically get it done? Then what keeps you from doing the things you know that you need to do? If you know that you need to do them, no question, then what keeps you from doing them? The answer is that there *is* a question in your mind. Your why has not been answered satisfactorily. You are not convinced. How much better would life be if you didn't have your back to the wall before you dealt with your life challenges?

Purposed performance involves *choosing* a course in life rather than waiting for life to happen to you. Motivation is the answer for salesmen helping people choose products or services. The real question isn't price. It is their motivation. How badly do they want or need what you are selling? It is also the answer for parents dealing with teenagers who are making bad choices. Again, the real issue is their motivation. Are teens more motivated by the gain they anticipate in their decision or by the pain they might experience as a result? I am not talking about parents issuing emotional threats. I am talking about parents *Purposed performance involves choosing a course in life rather than waiting for life to happen to you.* who are strong enough to help their children deal with the choices they make and then are committed enough to be there to love them through their consequences. The same applies to managers dealing with negative employees. It is all about their motivation. Negative people must be given the opportunity to choose. Is it more important to them to continue to whine, blame, and divide, or to continue to be employed? They may choose to take their act somewhere else and they should be allowed to make that choice. Managers should not be firing people. Instead, they should be helping people choose wisely on a daily basis.

Some people mistakenly view motivation as one of those "warm and fuzzy" issues. Unfortunately, too many of those people are in roles where people performance is being directly influenced. Motivation is not a soft issue. It is a rock-solid hard issue. It is the primary force behind morale and performance in the workplace. It is the energy behind marriage and family. Motivation holds both the question and the answer. And, once again, it is your choice.

It all begins with the power of your why.

It is important to note that the Purposed Performance Paradigm we mentioned earlier involves crossing the line of discipline to a more responsive life performance. Crossing that line, and staying across the line, hinges on the depth of passion and conviction in your reason why. The more convicted your thinking is, the more committed you will be in your new life disciplines. And it all begins with the power of your why. Get ready, choose this progression, and begin to discover what really makes things happen for you.

PHILOSOPHY: **PERSONAL AND SPIRITUAL**

Motivation is *your* responsibility. It doesn't belong to your parents, your manager, your coach, your spouse, your company, or your church. In a spiritual sense, you cannot be a grandchild of God. You can have only a first-generational relationship. It is personal to you. That brings us back to the issue of *why*.

Organizational Mission

Some years ago, the concept of *mission* seemed to dawn upon corporate

America. I have often given Tom Peters credit for the popularization of the thought through his incredibly popular book *In Search of Excellence*. Although I have since heard Tom repent for that book, I think he is being a little hard on himself. There were, and are, some excellent insights in the book, although it has been victimized by the most rapidly changing business landscape the world has ever known. I do believe, however, the mission concept fell short as it does with most organizations in America. Think about it: What value is there for an organization, actually an executive few within an organization, to create a mission statement for the organization as a whole when the people who make up that organization have no mission statement of their own? While I do see value in executive direction and vision, I believe it is most often doomed from the beginning because of the poor self-esteem of employees who do not see enough value in themselves to warrant a personal sense of mission.

If the people don't have a sense of ownership, they will not accept responsibility.

The empowerment movement was a great idea imagined by an executive few and then launched upon an employee community who had no sense of, nor desire for, personal power and responsibility. When will we come to understand that if the people don't have a sense of ownership, they will not accept responsibility? I was once asked to speak to an organization dealing with morale and performance issues, and I was brought in to help them get back on track. In one employee meeting, I asked if they had a shared corporate mission statement. I quickly got a nonverbal yes, so I proceeded to ask the people what it said. The reaction was predictable. I asked five or six specific people, who had no idea, and no one around them volunteered. The atmosphere began to get a little tense, so I suggested a break during which time I asked one of the managers to get me a copy of the statement for our review. At the end of the break, he didn't come back. About twenty minutes into the session, he came walking in with a framed statement and a red face. It seemed that their only copy had fallen down behind a copy machine and no one had missed it. Can you believe it? I know you can. Many of you know exactly what these people felt. As we explored it together, we found that the original statement had been created some eight years before. It wasn't a bad statement; it was just no longer relevant or representative. I discovered that less than half of the "now" organization had been around eight years ago. They did not know where the mission statement was; they did not know what it said; and they had no real insight into its origin. Therefore, it wasn't their mission.

Personal Mission

True organizational mission needs to be a blended effort between executive vision and employee commitment. Most people I encounter have never thought about the need for a personal mission statement. One young woman at a seminar came up to me looking distressed and began to earnestly explain that she was only twenty-two. She continued to say that she had never considered having a personal mission statement. She had never thought seriously of herself as making a difference to anything. In reality, she had never seriously thought much. That is not meant to be a criticism, rather an observation. In his great book, *The Road Less Traveled and Beyond*, Scott Peck notes that the greatest problem facing America today is that we have no time to think. I agree, but I believe it goes even further. We are not encouraged to believe that as individuals we are valuable enough to put a mission statement in place. We don't make time for it because we don't see it as being essential to our lives. And we wonder why so many people deal with motivation and morale problems!

There is another reason. We have not been taught how to formulate a mission statement. We don't even know where to start in the thought process. On one occasion, a small organization engaged me to help them develop a mission statement. I began with them the way I do with every group. I asked the owner to think about what motivated him then to write down his reason why. I next asked each member of his team to do the same. Why did they work for this man? Why did they choose to do what they were doing with almost half of their waking hours? I gave them about an hour during our session to work on their individual statements.

One team member happened to be the newest, as well as the youngest, of the group. I could tell she was having a hard time with the assignment. In fact, in the entire time she had not been able to put two words together on paper. When we came together as a group, I asked everyone to identify their reason why and I began with her. She was a little embarrassed by it all, but there was a method to my madness. I asked her what kept her from having an answer.

She said simply, "I don't know why I am here."

I asked her if she had ever had trouble with personal motivation, and it was obvious that I had struck a chord.

Tears came to her eyes and she said, "All the time."

I tried to lighten things up by asking her if she was independently wealthy. When she said no, I asked her if she had any trust accounts supporting her. She again said no, and then before I could ask my next question she said that she was a single mom. I asked about her child, and she said that her daughter was eighteen months old. I asked her name, and she said her name was Ally. So I told her to write Ally's name on her sheet. Ally was her reason why. It wasn't the "cause" of the profession that motivated her. It was the need of a child who was totally depending on her for support. I asked her to talk a little about how important Ally was to her. You should have seen the passion in her eyes and heard the motivation in her voice. You see, she simply needed to connect every day with the motivation in her own life, not in someone else's. Corporate America needs to get in touch with the motivation of its people.

Corporate America needs to get in touch with the motivation of its people.

They need to plug in to what makes their people get up and go—or they will get up and go! Some may need help getting in touch with it for the first time. Then once they've identified their personal motivation, they should remind themselves of that choice every day.

PERSPECTIVE: VALUABLE AND DISTINCTIVE

No one can do what you do. You cannot be replaced. I am not saying that someone else cannot do your job. I am saying that no one can do what you do the way you do it, because no one else in the world is you! You have to believe it. Every day you have more than one reason for doing what you do and for doing it well, but one of the most significant reasons is that you make a distinctive contribution to the world around you.

It is not uncommon for me to meet people in organizations across America whom I call "just a" people. I call them that because that is the way they introduce themselves to me. I will say, "Hi. I'm Allen Tappe." They will then say, "Oh. I'm just a receptionist." Or, "I am just a temp." "Just a" people see themselves as people who can be done without. If that were true, they should never have been done with. Every single person in your organization, family, or community must be valued for the contribution they are making and for the potential they have for making one.

I met a young man once who responded to my introduction by saying that he was "just a runner." I asked him if he ran the 100 meters, the 400 meters, or what? He smiled and said no, that he delivers things to people. I asked him to whom, and he said to the customers of the company. I said, "You make contact with the customers of this organization every single day?" He looked at me a bit bewildered and said yes. I said, "Then, you might be one of the most significant people I have had the opportunity to meet in this company." I then told him one of the most important lessons I had learned in my professional life:

I began my professional career teaching tennis. I played tennis in college and taught for a number of years but quickly came to grips with the fact that I would never make the kind of money in tennis that I aspired to make. When George, one of the several different businessmen I was teaching, asked me about my plans for the future, I told him I didn't have a clue. He asked me if I had ever thought about going into the mortgage banking business. After I explained that I had no idea that there was such a thing as the mortgage banking business, he offered me an opportunity to apprentice with him. George was pretty convincing, and I was pretty easy to convince, so I entered mortgage banking. I had to get a haircut and a suit, both of which were new experiences for me. On my first day of work, I was delighted to receive the keys to my new company car—a hot, yellow Buick Skylark, filled with gas and everything. It was several days before I figured out my position in the organization.

I was the "gopher." People would tell me to go here, go there. I went all day long. In the mornings, I drove to Dallas to the Veterans Administration and to the Federal Housing Administration. In the afternoons I went to Fort Worth and the Federal Housing Administration office for that part of the Metroplex. In between time, I was asked to go to title companies, real estate companies, and to other places where deliveries needed to be made.

After a few weeks of that, I went into George's office and told him I was ready to move on. I will never forget his response.

He said, "So, you have learned all you can learn in this position, huh?"

I told him I had mastered the trips to Dallas and to Fort Worth. I had even mastered the parking problem by fashioning a delivery sign for my car window.

He then posed a question I will never forget: "Have you met all of the people that you need to meet at FHA and the VA?"

I didn't know what to say because I didn't really know what he was talking about. I didn't know it was my job. He explained that it wasn't my job, but rather it was my opportunity. It was a major epiphany in my life. Every day I was approaching my life as though I was making no significant difference, when in reality every day presented a personal opportunity I was not even seeing. By the way, thank you, George, for your investment in me!

How do you see each day in your life? Do you see it as another twenty-four hours to experience and endure? Or do you see it as a unique gift that holds great purpose and possibility? The difference in perspective is more than semantics. The way you approach each day of your life reflects just how much you believe you are worth. It reveals how much difference you purpose to make in the world around you.

I once was asked to speak to a group of elementary school teachers who taught "at risk" children. Their parents were typically doing everything they could to survive, so the children were pretty much left on their own, making it particularly challenging for the teachers. I arrived a little early for my meeting, although school had already been dismissed for the day. The children became a welcoming party for me as I walked onto the campus. Because of their family disadvantages, they really had no place to go. They wanted to know who I was, where I was going, and what I was going to say to their teachers. I loved it. These kids may have been "at risk," but they were not at all shy.

As we talked, several of the children asked me if I was going to meet Mr. Moreno. I told them I was sure that I would. So when I was introduced to the assembly of teachers, I thanked them for the invitation and told them of my visit with their children. When I then asked for Mr. Moreno to identify himself, I noticed the teachers whispering to each other, and then the principal explained to me that Mr. Moreno was the school custodian. I asked them if we could invite Mr. Moreno to talk to us all about how to build a meaningful relationship with these children.

Through conversation with the teachers I discovered that Mr. Moreno was one special man who had an incredibly positive impact upon the students of this school. Someone who heard me tell this story shared with me that in his school district the educator of the year was one of the custodians. How does that happen? It obviously goes beyond job description. Right down the street in the same school district you could, no doubt, find someone who would resent having to play the role of custodian. We definitely need more Mr. Morenos in this world, who have a sense of purpose and mission that goes well beyond mere job description.

PERFORMANCE: PASSION-FILLED AND PRIORITY-DRIVEN

When you see yourself through eyes that have been awakened to the reality of your divine heritage and purposed destiny, each day will look a little brighter. Even when circumstances seem to dictate otherwise, your convictions will produce light on your daily landscape, much like the gifted artist Thomas Kinkade distinctively does in each work he produces. You will communicate an infectious and attractive message to the world around you.

I cannot tell you how many people I talk to who are looking for something else to do with their lives. They seem to believe that if they could just change their profession, everything would get better. The reality is that if you do not see purpose for yourself right where you are, you will probably not see purpose for yourself wherever you go. I am not saying that pursuing a profession that better suits your strengths or your needs is inappropriate. I am just saying that moving, in and of itself, is not the key. If you leave one company because of a few people in that company, you will probably run into their cousins in the next company. You simply have to deal with your situation. Your personal reason why must be strong enough to deal with whatever each day brings.

Wherever you are, whatever you are doing, there is meaning to be found in it. You are unique. You bring a distinctive presence and have purpose-filled reason for doing what you do. So, what can you say or do in each of your days to communicate yourself with passion to the world around you?

One Sunday morning, as the guest speaker in a somewhat small, rural church, I was asked to speak to a combined adult class, which included most of the church's adults. As I began to meet people before class, they kept asking if I had met one particular man. I could not tell you his name, but I can tell you that to this day his story has had an impact on me. One by one members related how the gentleman had been responsible for telling them about Jesus. He had personally introduced them to a force that had changed their lives. I was told that the same was true for the majority of that community. I could not wait to meet this man. I was sure that I was about to meet one powerful personality. In fact, I met a meek, ordinary looking man, but the passion I saw in his eyes told me he was far from ordinary.

A mail carrier for thirty years, he passed up opportunities to advance his career because delivering mail gave him the chance to encounter the people he felt called to meet. He not only delivered mail, he delivered a message.

Staying Motivated

Being motivated and *staying* motivated can be two very different things. You can have a strong, passionate why for life. You can even see yourself as making a distinctive difference in the lives of others. But sometimes it is hard to stay motivated. Some days the feelings simply aren't there. When those days come—and they do— here are some things for you to remember:

• *Don't follow the lead of your feelings.* I am not saying to deny your feelings. In fact, your feelings may be sending you signals that you need to heed concerning your health and your well-being. I am just saying, don't buy into the idea that feeling down is evidence that you are down. Don't let feeling depressed tell you that you are depressed. Let your feelings say what they need to say, and then choose to respond to them in a way that is in keeping with who you are.

• *Get out into the light.* If it is at all possible, get out into the light God intends for you to experience. It is amazing the difference the warmth of the sun can have upon the way we feel. Where natural light isn't available, find a bright place to be. Remember, things that you feel will impact how you feel and, ultimately, how you will act.

• *Find people who are up.* When you are having a difficult day, it is best to find someone who isn't. Team is a remarkable force when we put it to work. You need to have people on your life team who will be there for you when you need them. Of course, the relationship needs to be reciprocal.

• *Listen to music that is up.* It is amazing the impact that music can have on your life. Listen to music that lifts your heart. Listen to music that speaks to your spirit. When you are feeling down, listen to something that can reach beneath those feelings. Music has penetrating spiritual power that is hard to explain but delightful to experience.

• *Don't expect too much from yourself.* Give yourself a break. Being human has some definite disadvantages. One of them is that we will have down times. Part of dealing with those times and getting over them involves accepting them as being part of life's process. I'm not talking about giving in to how you feel. I am, however, talking about respecting how you feel.

Motivation Is the Issue

In order to do life on purpose, you have to be motivated. It's true for individuals, and it's true for teams. Your reason why must be clear. It must become your passion. Even so, you will need to remind yourself of it daily. It's so easy for us to become distracted. And keep in mind, it's not a long journey from being distracted to being distraught.

Believing in *what* you are doing is equally essential. You just have to believe that you are making a difference with the way you are investing half of your life. There is little question that you're making that difference. It has probably been some time, however, since you let yourself reflect upon just how much of a difference you are making. You have to stay reminded in order to stay motivated.

Knowing *where* all of this effort is leading is an interdependent part of this motivation equation. Confidence in the difference you are making will be reflected in the progress that you see yourself making. To see that reflection clearly, you must have some sense of destination. But that destination won't be completely clear because there will be so much to learn along the way. Your vision of where you believe you are heading, however, will work for you. Keep it before you so it can.

TAKE THE CHALLENGE

Here is an exercise to help you become clear about motivation in your life. Take some personal time and write the answer to the following questions. Remember, your answers do not need to impress anyone but you. They are not for show. Further, they can be as long-term or as short-term in nature as you would like to make them. Once again, they are for you; reconsider these questions regularly. As life changes, many times your personal motivation must change as well.

- What are you doing with your life and what difference do you see yourself making? *(What is your purpose?)*
- Why are you choosing to do life the way you do? *(What is your mission?)*
- Where are you heading as a result of your life choices? *(What is your vision?)*

These questions can be used by individuals and by organizations alike. Where they are used by organizations, I suggest they be considered in light of the answers provided by each individual member of the organization. Let each person see the spirit of his/her mission reflected in the mission statement of the organization.

Motivation is not some warm and fuzzy, soft and fluffy, issue. It is the most important issue of your life and for the life of any organization of people. Thinking about it is not easy; it's not really even natural. It will, however, provide the energy you need to live life powerfully and purposefully.

AFFIRMATIONS

I believe in myself.
I believe in my mission.
I know I make a difference.
I know where I am going.
I have a great support team.
I am committed.

THE
COMMUNICATION
CONNECTION

I'll never forget the scene: The crowded streets of New York City near Times Square. I've never seen so many people in my life! You couldn't walk without bumping into someone or turn around without someone trying to sell you something. Yet no one was communicating. Everyone was talking, but no one was listening.

People are all around us—we run into them every single day. We talk to one another all the time. The technological support we have for making connection has never been more available. Telephone, telegraph, and mail service have become old news. Mobile communication, once a luxury, is now the rule. We connect via mobile telephone, e-mail, fax, voicemail, beepers, pagers, tele-conferencing, videoconferencing, and long-distance service that makes every call a local call. Intranet connection and networks within organizations have served to make the transfer of information systematic. We've never been more connected, technologically speaking. Yet all of the technological support in the world can't meet the challenges we face in connecting as people.

The testimony is overwhelming. We don't know how to make a healthy connection with the people around us. History bears the scars of people who have been separated by every form of prejudice imaginable. Racial discrimination, civil war, social arrogance, intellectual pride, and on and on the list can go of our communication barriers. What we do not understand or relate to, we judge. So condemnation and separation become our answer. Dynamics like that make division inevitable.

We don't have to look back to see our obvious challenge. Just look around: Divorce has become more the rule than the exception. Families are being fractured. Children are being abused every day by parents who don't know how to connect. Schools have come under siege. Metal detectors line the corridors. Students are shooting other students, and teachers fear their students. Churches haven't dodged the bullet either. Brothers are divided against brothers. Churches split. People are hurt and faith is damaged. Communities have lost their definition. Who is your neighbor? The banks and barbershops no longer play host to communities of people. There seems to be no dependable place to connect. And so we go behind our walls and try to protect ourselves.

Because people feel they no longer have home and school, church and community to depend on, communication has never been worse. *It's fear that* The institutions we depend on for our connection are not *separates* delivering, and we are simply not adjusting to the challenge. *children* Relationships suffer. Companies assume that the people they hire *from adults.* know how to communicate and connect with the people around them. Unfortunately, that assumption results in conflict, and morale in the workplace has never been worse. I sometimes hear frustrated executives say, "They're adults. They should be able to communicate." My response is swift and simple, "Because they're adults they have learned how *not* to communicate." It's fear that separates children from adults. We come into this world without fear. As we grow older, we experience life and learn the things that we need to fear and avoid.

It's time for us to make connection. We need to set aside our fears and meet one another on the field of discovery and healing. Our future and the future of our children depend on our learning the art of effective communication. It won't happen by accident. Nor will it be a natural happening. Connecting must be done *on purpose.* Maybe this progression will work for you.

PHILOSOPHY: DESTINY AND DISCOVERY

We were not created to be alone, nor were we created to be separated. We are relational beings. It's part of our destiny to connect with one another. To the degree that we are out of touch with others, we are out of touch with our destiny as human beings. Connecting with other human beings, in many ways, reflects a deeper connection, and that connection is within you. Loving God, loving the people in your world, and loving yourself are all part of the same package. Any part missing in the equation reflects deficiency in the other parts.

Spiritual connection is the initial and essential element to any real connection you might hope to make with either yourself or the people around you. It's amazing how long it has taken us to realize that. The most obvious illustration of this discovery has been found through the work of the anonymous communities. The "Twelve-Step" programs originated with a couple of guys struggling with the destructive effects of alcohol addiction. Alcoholics Anonymous has now become the journey for all those who recognize compulsion as being a life battle. This step-by-step approach to reconnecting with your world is a trip we all should make. An early step in the program is the recognition of the need for a greater Power outside of yourself to take over. That recognition is foundational to overcoming. Communication with others begins with the connection we must make with the One who made it all possible.

Relationship with self is the most challenging human relationship we have to face because it's constant. You may have heard the expression "familiarity breeds contempt." We live with the potential for a contemptuous storm raging within us all of the time. Earlier I mentioned that the quality of your self-talk often disqualifies you from being a positive life force for yourself. We learn to be critical of ourselves at an early age. We could spend a lot of time examining the potential sources for that destructive development, but the reality is that looking for something or someone to blame is largely a waste of time. Rather, we need to call upon our power of choice and the recognition that we need to learn to love and value ourselves. While we can't change what has been said or done, we can change the emotional "tapes" we choose to listen to on a daily basis. The self-criticism needs not only to stop, it needs to be replaced with the kind of positive communication that will motivate and encourage you. The Affirmations offered in each chapter may be a beginning for you in that regard.

While we can't change what has been said or done, we can change the emotional "tapes" we choose to listen to on a daily basis.

It isn't common for us to think much about having any real relationship with ourselves. In reality, a strong intrapersonal relationship, the relationship you have with you, is essential to any healthy relationship you might hope to have with others. A spiritual connection, complemented by a positive intrapersonal connection, will prepare you for making the interpersonal connections you need to make with others. Once we have established our need for people in our lives, we need to embrace the challenge of communicating with them. You can't wait for others to initiate the connection—the conviction and the commitment need to begin with you.

While working with one organization, I met a man who experienced an epiphany in this area. After one of our meetings, he introduced himself to me as a person who, at least initially, did not have a high regard for the role I was playing with his company. He admitted, however, that he had recently received a job review that suggested he was not connecting well with the people around him, and so he decided maybe he needed to give what I was saying a try.

I had exposed the group to an excellent little book by Alan Loy McGinnis called *Bringing Out the Best in People*. In it McGinnis does a great job of making a case for the mutual leadership capability and responsibility for all of us as human beings. He then suggests twelve rules for bringing out the best in people that he discovered from his study of a variety of contemporary and historical leaders. The first rule on his list is to "expect the best of those you lead." In introducing this thought, McGinnis briefly discusses the dynamic of self-fulfilling prophecy.

The man then told me that he decided to try out that first rule. So he picked out someone at work that he didn't like a lot; he didn't have to look far. He then began to go to this man and ask him how he was doing. He would ask about his family and his work. He said the man thought something was the matter with him. I asked him how it worked. He said that, as it turned out, he really liked the guy. He then said he picked someone else and did the same thing. The result was the same. He said that he was working on his third.

Then, he very seriously related to me just how frustrating it was to discover this late in life that he had been standing back *While effective* in judgment of the world around him instead of embrac- *communication* ing it. He told me that if I ever needed to have him *requires the work of* relate his story to others, he would do it. Well, now he *at least two, it must* has. *begin with the*

Communicating effectively with others is not only a *leadership of* challenge, it's a necessity. While effective communication *at least one.* requires the work of at least two, it must begin with the leadership of at least one. You are the only one you can control. You are the only one you can change. So fulfilling your destiny begins one person at a time. Recognizing the distinctive possibilities in the people around you makes each day an adventure in human discovery.

PERSPECTIVE: UNUSUAL AND UNCOMFORTABLE

Have you ever marveled at the weirdness in the people around you? Don't they just look and sound strange? Have you ever stopped to think that they are looking at you, as part of the world around them, and thinking the same thing? The truth is, everyone but me is just weird! Actually, the challenge begins with this idea. Our differences don't rest only in a few of the most obvious obstacles we might cite, like gender, age, and race. We are each unique and unusual to the world around us. Here is the point: All human communication is a cross-cultural experience.

Have you ever noticed how frustrated you get when you try to communicate with people who are foreign to you? They look different. They talk different. They speak a different language. Things don't necessarily mean the same thing to them that they mean to you. Be honest. How well do you think you communicate in these uncomfortable life situations? Have you ever noticed how you begin to talk a little slower and a little louder in an effort to break through?

Years ago, I faced a potentially career-ending struggle with my vocal cords. I developed nodes on my vocal cords and faced the possibility of risky surgery. Fortunately, the nodes were in the early stages of development, so my speech therapist suggested that an extended voice rest might prevent surgery. She stressed, however, that the rest needed to be complete. No whispering. No talking at all. Barbara and the girls loved it.

On one particular morning, I was at home by myself reading the classifieds when I found a truck that I had been looking for to pull my horse trailer. The dealership was close by, so I took my writing pad and I went with the mission of buying that vehicle. I am a buyer. I am not a shopper.

When I arrived on the lot, I found the truck immediately. It was exactly what I needed. A sales representative spotted me and was coming my way. When he was a few feet from me, I held up my hand to stop him, and I wrote on my pad that I wanted that truck.

He looked closely at what I had written and then looked up at me and shouted, "OKAY! I WILL HELP YOU GET THIS TRUCK!"

I couldn't believe it. I held up my pad and wrote on it, *"Voice rest, I can hear!"*

That was my first personal experience as a real victim of fear in cross-cultural communication.

I witnessed a similar incident that further exposes our difficulty in handling these awkward moments. A person who worked for me had two clients who both happened to be hearing impaired. In fact, they were both able to communicate effectively only through sign language. As I came by the office where they were working together, I heard my colleague talking to these two people in a loud voice. In fact, she was almost screaming. I asked her to join me in the hall for a moment. When she arrived, I asked her what she thought she was doing. She had no idea what I meant. I explained what I heard and wondered if she thought she was going to make a communication breakthrough with these two hearing-impaired people by screaming her message. The truth is that the more uncomfortable she got, the louder her voice grew.

So what happens to us? I believe fear is the major culprit. We fear what we can't understand. We also fear what we can't control. So, in effect, other people can be serious roadblocks in communication, because they all seem so weird to us, and because we can't control them, no matter how much we try to convince ourselves that we can.

We have to begin to see the world and the people around us through new eyes. We have to learn to treat them with the respect they deserve as distinctively created beings. We have to regard them as daily opportunities for discovery. The variety people bring to our day is incredible. You never know quite what to expect tomorrow because you will, no doubt, run into someone who is not you. They will look, think, and act differently. Your challenge, then, is to see each person as a positive life experience. The weirder they are, the more potential there is in the relationship. Choose *not* to put people in a box. And, above all, choose *not* to judge people through your eyes. As Stephen Covey puts it, "Seek first to understand." Try to look through their eyes. Try to discover the world that they see. When you begin to get their world in view, real communication can begin. Remember, diversity is not an issue; it is your reality!

PERFORMANCE: LISTEN AND LEARN

"So, what do I say?" That's the most common question asked by people seeking to become more effective communicators. And the question itself reveals the genesis of the challenge we face. Communication doesn't begin with what *you* have to say but rather with what *they* need to say. We put incredible pressure on ourselves when we imagine that what we say will make or break the relationship. In reality, effective communication involves both a process and a pattern.

> *Communication doesn't begin with what you have to say but rather with what they need to say.*

Communication is really a value statement. It says how much you value yourself and others—and how much you value the Power who made it all possible. It is a statement about how close you are to achieving your destiny. It won't just happen; it has to be done on purpose. It cannot be taken for granted any more than people can be taken for granted. It involves process, and it's best pursued through a pattern. It requires anticipation, and it works best through the proactive power of preparation. The final touch to the process involves something that separates professionals from amateurs in any area, and that something is practice.

"Practice makes perfect" is really not true. Practice in pursuit of perfection makes perfect. The importance of prethinking and paying attention to your communication challenges can't be overstated. Anticipation is the value you receive for tomorrow from paying attention to your challenges today. Once you begin to clarify expectations with regard to the relationships in your life, communication will become a positive experience, and real connection will be the result.

Before any effective connection can take place, the barriers have to come down. Never underestimate resistance in any communication effort. Remember, because of our uniqueness, fear and misunderstanding are lurking close by. The first step in the process is always to break down any barriers that might exist.

Have you ever tried to argue with someone who will not argue with you? Begin by letting them know that you are on their side. Assure them that you want no dividing walls to exist. You can accomplish that simply by mastering a pattern in communication.

Mastering a Purposed Pattern of Communication

The steps to this pattern will correspond to the process that is being developed.

Affirm the Person. In order to facilitate breaking down the barriers, the first step in the pattern is to affirm the person you want to connect with. Here are a couple of examples of what I mean. Perhaps you are communicating with someone who is not happy about the way you have handled a particular situation. Your point of beginning needs to be something like: "I want you to know that getting this right is really important to me, so I am glad you were willing to bring it to my attention." Don't get hung up on the words. You will need to choose your own. But don't underestimate the point. If barriers are not broken down in the beginning, any communication is going to be inhibited at best. Maybe you want to reconnect with a friend. You might start by saying, "I want to begin by reminding you that time can never destroy the relationship we have built." The point is to deal positively and on purpose with whatever tension that might be in the air.

Ask a Directional Question. While each part of the process is significant, this next step might well be the most significant. Clarify the situation and the direction the conversation needs to take. Never assume anything! Don't assume that you know what others are thinking. Don't assume that they will know what direction the conversation needs to go. Don't assume that they will say anything. Assume a leadership position in the relationship. Being a leader does not suggest that you control but rather that you ensure communication. How you lead, however, is the key. Remember this: The person asking the question is always leading.

The person asking the question is always leading.

So the next step in the pattern is to clarify by asking a question. Of course, once you have asked the question, the really important work of listening begins. The worst thing you can do in seeking to make connection with another person is to ask a question and then not listen to their answer. That means don't cut them off. Don't answer the question for them. Ask the question and then listen actively.

The question you ask should come from a desire to keep the conversation on point. Always ask open-ended questions. Ask *what, when, where,* and *how* questions, but stay away from *why* questions. They are motive questions and may take you someplace you don't want to go.

Periodically, I lose my mind and question Barbara about why she has either done or not done something with our bookkeeping. She will typically respond to my ill-placed question by saying something like, "I guess it's just because I am so stupid. Maybe you ought to do it." That's my cue that I have made a serious error in judgment. Asking good questions communicates your interest in the thoughts and the input of the other person.

*A **side note for selling professionals:** The number-one complaint about sales people across the country is that you talk too much. Many of you have been falsely led to believe that as long as you are talking you are in control. Nothing could be further from the truth. To begin with, never have we had so little reason in our country to trust anyone about anything. The more you talk, the more reason you are giving people to believe that you have something to hide. The key is to ask and listen—listen and learn. Put other people and their needs on center stage. Let them know that they are going to be the point of this conversation.*

Lead Through Consensus. Returning to the process involves the application of what you have heard in response to your question. The next step in the pattern is for you to lead through consensus.

Once you have heard their input, your challenge as a leader becomes creating consensus and agreement. Take what you have heard and feed back to them thoughts designed to create that agreement. You might say something like, "Based upon what you have said, I would recommend that we pursue this course." Or, you might say "Your insights have helped me better understand what you are trying to achieve, so let me recommend."

The point is, you are being responsive to what they have said. You are letting them know that their input is valued. Once again, the worst thing you can do, next to not listening, is to give no credibility to what they have just said. It will come across as though you never intended to pay any attention to them. Even if you do not agree, affirm them for answering your question, and then acknowledge your differences. You can then begin to search for a place of agreement or even compromise. Achieving compromise is a result of strength more often than weakness.

Achieving compromise is a result of strength more often than weakness.

Clear the Way. The final step in the process is vital to the ongoing relationship and to furthering communication in that relationship. Always conclude your time with a person by opening the door to the next opportunity you hope to enjoy. Particularly when there has been some kind of tension or compromise as a result of the conversation, communication needs to take place that will serve to clear the air. In fact, the next step in the pattern is to clear the way and set the stage for the next communication.

At the conclusion of a particularly tense meeting, you might say something like, "I really appreciate the way you have helped us get to the next level in our relationship. I look forward to what the future will bring." Or when compromise has been successfully achieved, you might say, "It really means a lot to be able to work with someone who understands and appreciates harmony. I look forward to our next working opportunity." The goal is to make sure there are no lingering impediments to the future of the relationship.

Prepare to Connect

Knowing the process and having a pattern puts you into a new place as a communicator. You are now equipped to prepare. The only thing missing is what you need to prepare. If you hope to make purposed connections with people around you, you have to pay attention, look for signals, and anticipate the challenges to come.

The best form of preparation is always anticipation.

If you can anticipate a challenge, then you can prepare to meet it. If you are prepared to meet it, then you will be more confident and effective in the midst of it. The best form of preparation is always anticipation.

Ted Williams is arguably the best hitter baseball has ever known. The key to his success as a hitter, no doubt, rested in his incredible vision. I have read that from the time the ball left the pitcher's hand, before it had traveled any distance at all, he could tell you not only which pitch was being thrown but which way the seams of the ball were turning. Imagine the advantage to hitting a ball being thrown ninety miles per hour, if you could anticipate where it was going and what it was going to look like.

The same is true in communicating with people. If you can anticipate challenges, you can prethink your responses and be better prepared for meeting the challenges. Some would refer to this as scripting. All of us use scripts in our communication. You say the same kinds of things over and over again. It just may be time to change your script.

It had been a lousy day: too much to do, not enough time, not enough resources or support. The telephone rang and it was Barbara asking me to stop on the way home and pick up some chicken. We had a number of teens hanging around the house at suppertime (a universal truth) and she said it would be a lot of help if I would bring something home on my way. Fried chicken just seemed to be the easiest. Maybe her request engaged the male spirit to provide food for the family, I don't know, but I did as I was told. My challenge was simple. Or, at least I thought it was. What I expected to be a run-of-the-mill experience, however, soon became something much more.

I placed my order and then walked out with about forty dollars' worth of chicken in two large bags. Ten minutes later, I was finally home after a long day of trying to "get it all done." Even with all of the frustrations of the day, I had managed to bring home the food for the family. Or at least I thought I had. Then, I made the fateful discovery that would cap off an already frustrating day. The "chicken people" had left several pieces of chicken out of my order. When Barbara asked why I had not gotten enough chicken for the teen challenge we faced, I impatiently and defensively explained to her that I had gotten my part right. It was "the chicken people" who had messed up. This was more than I could take in one day. I picked up the telephone. The "chicken people" would pay! Barbara tried to calm me and protect me from myself. I told her that this call was just what the doctor ordered. How can "chicken people" mess up chicken anyway?

The young woman who answered the telephone received me graciously on behalf of her company and then asked if there was anything she could do to help. I replied with a judgmental and harsh, "I doubt it! Let me speak to your manager."

In a short moment, a woman identifying herself as the manager came on the line and followed the young woman's inquiry with the same question. I once again pronounced judgment with a firm "I doubt it!" I then said, "My name is Allen Tappe, which means nothing to you, but here is the question: If a person spends forty dollars on chicken in your place of business, is that a lot of money?"

I knew I had her there, or at least I thought I did, until she replied graciously but with confidence: "Mr. Tappe, if a person spends one dollar in my store, that is a lot of money."

That really set me back a little. Her answer was much better than I had expected. But I recovered and returned to my mission of venting for all of the fast food challenges I had ever faced in the past.

"Well, I spent forty dollars, and when I got home my order was incorrect. Chicken was left out of the order. How do 'chicken people' mess chicken up anyway? It isn't rocket science. You take the chicken ordered and simply put it into the bag!"

I really unloaded on her. She may not have deserved it all, but she got it anyway. Throughout my diatribe, she never once interrupted or corrected me. She simply let me get everything completely out of my system.

When I had basically run out of gas, she began, "Mr. Tappe, I want to thank you for your call. Most people don't call, and as a result we don't get the opportunity to let them know how sorry we are. Treating our customers so unprofessionally is not our goal. I know this won't fix anything, but would it be okay with you for us to deliver the chicken to your house?"

I couldn't believe it. Sensing something unusual was in the works, Barbara wanted to know what was happening. I held up my hand to put her on hold while I tried to recover somehow. All I could say with a pitiful, broken voice was, "Sure."

She then got the details of my order and my address and followed by saying, "Mr. Tappe, I want to thank you once again for your call. Without your call, we would never have had the opportunity to let you know how sorry we are. Nor would we have had the opportunity to begin the process of earning your business back. I look forward to meeting you and your family when you return to our store."

I was in shock. Barbara couldn't wait to hear what had happened. I explained to her that they were going to deliver it to us. She joined me in my disbelief but wondered why I just stood there with a skeptical look on my face. After a few moments in thought, I said, "I wonder if they left that chicken out on purpose?" It was quite a performance.

There are several points to be made through this little story. Think about the implications for your life and for your business:

1. *A professional response can convert the most emotional critic into an even more committed customer.* I really wondered for a moment if the whole thing had been orchestrated. Think about it. Was I a more committed customer before or after the incident?

2. *An anticipated challenge can provide opportunity for the performance of a lifetime.* This was obviously not the first time an angry customer had called with an order that had been messed up. Do you think this woman just thought of this response off of the top of her head? No way. This was a well constructed script and a well-practiced performance.

3. *Preparation for an anticipated challenge produces great confidence in the midst of the challenge.* These people were not stressed by my call. From the one who greeted me to the one who treated me, they were ready. Now, think about the impact that kind of preparation has on reducing stress in the work place and improving morale.

I love this story. I remember it and tell it often because of the message it conveys. I hope that you will take the time to put into practice the concepts you have just experienced through my experience with "the chicken people." Thank you to all of the people who anticipate and prepare for life-challenged people like me!

TAKE THE CHALLENGE

Here is a challenge for you. Identify two people with whom you have your greatest communication challenges. Anticipate your next meetings with them and identify the challenges that exist between you. Write out for yourself a script involving the process and pattern you have just been taught. Remember to:

1. Affirm the person.
2. Ask a directional question.

3. Lead through consensus.

4. Clear the way.

Make it your script. Put it in your words. Practice it a number of times until you know it and feel confident with it. Then, pay attention to the difference it makes in those relationships as you approach them with the confidence that only preparation can bring. You might even write down the results, as you perceive them to be. Remember, communication is no real option. It is a connection you must make if you are going to live life on purpose.

AFFIRMATIONS

I recognize the One who is my Power.
I will speak to myself with respect.
I will connect with the people around me.
I will listen and I will learn.
I will anticipate and I will prepare.
I will practice and I will deliver.

CREATIVE
CONFLICT

I have a friend who is a physician who says that at the end of a stressful day, she doesn't want to have to make one more decision. She wants her evening to be decided for her. Of course, that puts a lot of pressure on both her and her family, because when she gets home conflict is always there to welcome her at the door. Unfortunately, families don't function without facing conflict—and dealing with it. To harmonize family responsibilities with professional responsibilities is a tremendous challenge for us all. Decision making can be avoided only a short time without serious consequences. And the peace you hoped to gain will be only short-lived.

How do you handle conflict? How do you think the majority of the world handles it? After asking this question to literally thousands of people across this country, I can tell you confidently that most people's answer is "avoid it." The paradox is that the world seems to be doing its best to avoid something we encounter every single day. And organizations across America wonder why morale seems to be an ever-present dilemma.

To recognize the prevalence of conflict in life, I want to define it for you. I believe that conflict occurs every time we face a situation that requires making a decision or a choice. Think about it. How often have you gotten into an unpleasant altercation over the choice of a restaurant like Barbara and I do, or over the choice of a movie? Obviously, the nature of the challenges we face and the choices we make must take on different levels of importance for our lives, but all day long, we face them. Priority choices in the workplace become one of the most wearing and paralyzing of all. There is always more to do than there is time to get it done, so what do you choose? The real question is, who will choose? Will it be you or will you be a victim of someone else's choosing?

Have you ever found yourself running away from a problem? Maybe you have left a job because of the jerk you had to work for or with. Running away from a conflict will almost always just delay the inevitable until another, and usually more dramatic or inconvenient time in your life.

I recently spent some time with a young woman who will soon be receiving her undergraduate degree. She was relating to me her frustration with all of the heavy decisions she had to face. As a result, she was preparing herself for graduate school as a fallback. I certainly do not discourage advanced degree studies, but I do think that many young people stay in school just to avoid tough choices.

Choices and decisions are at the heartbeat of conflict. Life can pivot on our choices, and so often the weight of the responsibility can be overwhelming. It certainly is exacerbated when we go into each day of life dreading the challenges we have before us.

Conflict in life is reality, and I believe it's a force that has been framed wrong from day one. For so many of us, conflict is synonymous with fighting—we have heard it from the day we were born. Our conflicts either resulted in pain or were avoided all together. Something has to change if we are ever going to experience life with all of its intended joy. Something has to change for us to be able to accept the new daily expectations we face in the workplace. Conflict must be reframed as the powerful and positive force that it can be and be engaged on purpose every day. Maybe you will choose to think about it through the following progression.

PHILOSOPHY: POWER AND POSSIBILITY

Conflict is power. There is no question that in the presence of conflict, potential exists. Think about some of the things we value most in life. If you look closely, you will recognize the creative presence of conflict. Nature itself teaches us that

Conflict is power.

lesson. In his book entitled *The Magic of Conflict*, Thomas Crum explores this question in some depth. If you consider the formation of the diamond, you will recognize the essential need for pressure. If you study the development of a pearl, you will encounter the reality of friction. If you examine the formations of the Grand Canyon, you will discover the years of erosion. On and on, nature testifies to the power of conflict.

Any mother can tell you about the conflict involved in childbirth. The birth of our firstborn provided one of those conflictive moments for us. Certainly more for Barbara than for me, but I have learned that it is really difficult to sit by and watch our loved ones in pain or afraid. After hours in labor, Barbara was told she must have an emergency Caesarian section. The surgery itself was successful, and Angela was born with minimal distress. Unfortunately, anesthesia was improperly administered: Barbara felt the entire thing but was unable to move or cry out. Her pain was indescribable. I was afraid that she would be scarred emotionally. But from the moment Angela was placed in her arms, my fears were dispelled. She was so beautiful and such a blessing. Through the pain of that unexpected conflict, a bond was forged that remains to this day. Mothers understand the depth of love that comes through the conflict of bringing new life into the world.

Angela has grown into an equally loving mother herself. Yet she would be the first to tell you that she has encountered great conflict along the way—some of it as a consequence of her choosing and some of it just because. Along the way, because of her choices, Angela became a teenage mother. I can't relate to you the pain and despair Angela experienced as she watched her childhood snatched from her. I can tell you, however, that as a result of that conflictive time in her life, this world has been blessed with a young lady—Savannah Hope—who has the potential to change the world. Angela has also used her experience to help many other young women work through the same challenges she faced. She has blessed others through the power and potential of conflict in her life.

Many years ago, I had my own life-changing experiences in "birthing" a kidney stone. Never in my life have I experienced such pain. I have always been blessed with excellent health, and so this was unfamiliar territory for me. When the stone failed to pass, it had to be extracted. I don't even want to begin to share what that meant. Let your imagination run wild. Fortunately, I was knocked out. Then because of surgical complications, an emergency nephrostomy had to be performed in which a tube was placed straight through my back to relieve my kidney. Over the course of several weeks, two lithotripsy procedures were performed. I know that others have had it far worse than I did, but that is not the point. The point is, through the conflict of that experience I learned to value good health. I saw just how quickly life can change, and my appreciation for the most basic bodily function increased immediately.

During the first career chapter of my life, I found myself managing a mortgage-lending branch office. Three employees were my responsibility, and I was fond of them all. On one occasion, a customer new to our organization came into our office really upset. He began to berate one of the women on my team, so I stepped out of my office to intercede. I invited him into my office where, behind closed doors, we proceeded to dramatically express our mutual disapproval of each other. It got loud—so much so that the women on my team were worried that they might have to call security. Somewhere in the fight, though, we both just started laughing. It suddenly became apparent to both of us just how stupid we were being. Out of that rather inauspicious beginning grew a relationship that has lasted a lifetime.

Conflict has creative power that can create relationships that will forever be unique because of the heat with which they ignite.

Conflict is a value-producing power that is just waiting for your response.

In itself, conflict is not positive or negative but carries the potential for both. That is what makes it so powerful. Conflict is a value-producing power that is just waiting for your response. Trying to avoid conflict is akin to avoiding life and all of its relationships. If you think about it, each morning promises unique potential—you can be confident that you will face challenges that will require life-changing choices. Anticipate how your daily conflict will energize and testify to your personal power. Instead of avoiding conflict, celebrate it!

PERSPECTIVE: OPPORTUNITY AND RELATIONSHIP

You may have heard the story of the two shoe salesmen who were sent to Japan to sell shoes. One of the men called home almost immediately saying, "Get me out of here! These people don't wear shoes!" The other called the same day saying, "Send all of the shoes we have! No one has shoes over here!" It all depends on how you choose to see things.

If you embrace the mindset that conflict is power waiting for your personal response, then conflict always provides opportunity. You might not choose to see it that way, but it is always there. We are living in a time when change has become an almost constant topic of conversation. Most people seem to be against it as if that makes any difference. Like it or not, change is going to happen. Change is definitely in the conflict "family" and, as a result, change always produces something new. Without question, it produces drama in our lives because it involves a death of sorts. It means the end of one way of doing things and the beginning of a new way. It means the end of one style and the beginning of a new one. It marks the end of one chapter of life and the beginning of another. In his book *Lightning in a Bottle*, David Baum recommends that all leaders approach change in much the way that we approach grief. Change is a process that has its own stages, and people will move through them at their own pace.

Our choice, however, is not whether we are for or against change. Rather, it is with what spirit will we ultimately approach it. I'm convinced that God has a sense of humor. As a young man in the early '70s, I, like many, embraced the liberating mark of long hair. My father wore a "burr" haircut, if you can relate to that. Conflict was real in my house over that question. I stood my ground, though, and demanded my freedom—but it came at great cost. Now, race forward with me thirty years. I now have a haircut much like my father. Not, I must add, by choice. God has done it to me. So what do you do? By the way, people around you won't always make it easy. I recently saw a woman I had not seen for twenty-five years. When she saw me her immediate response was, "What happened to your hair?" I have to confess that I was tempted to react to her with, "What happened to your body?" But I didn't. So what do you do when unwanted change comes your way? I have learned to embrace and enjoy it. I now sport what I like to call the "European look." It takes no time in the morning, and I don't have to have any hair paraphernalia. It is really great, and a lot of guys with the same hair challenge even ask me where I get my hair cut. I love it.

Aging is another issue we all have to face. You don't get a vote about that. I am afraid too much of the health movement is born out of a desire to escape natural aging and death. Studies have been done on the subject and the results are in: One out of one of us will die. Yet it still shocks our system, doesn't it? I once spoke in a program where I just casually mentioned the name of my high school in Hurst, Texas. On the front row, two young women began to squeal and say that they had attended the same high school. Now the intriguing thing was that we were miles away, in Gainesville, Florida. I took time to affirm them in the discovery of our mutual alma mater as several hundred people looked on. They then asked when I had graduated. When I said 1970, they looked stunned. A bit confused, I asked what was wrong with 1970. They then hit me with the news that they were not yet born in 1970. I immediately had them removed from the front row. So, what do you do? You go with it. You celebrate the fact that you get to see life through eyes of experience. You don't have to face many of the insane challenges and choices that face young people today. Choose to use your experience as an asset.

In the marketplace today, there is a premium being placed upon youth and education. Recent college graduates are being courted and placed into positions for which they have few if any practical qualifications. Many experienced people are being passed over for advancement. There is a lot of anger and frustration in the organizations across America because of this dynamic. Experienced people are angry. Young people are frustrated with the reaction of their older peers. So what do you do? See and seize the opportunity. Young people are being hired because educationally and emotionally they have been wired differently. When I graduated from high school, the most advanced technology we had was the IBM Selectric typewriter. It was great. I took a computer course in Fortran during my undergraduate years. Things have changed, huh? Young people today are learning to type by the sixth grade and are online and immersed in technology from day one. They are equipped emotionally for change. The experienced workers of America need to embrace these new minds and see them as their security for the near future. While you may miss a promotion or two, if you prove yourself to be the kind of valuable resource that can practically and positively mentor young minds, you will be secure in the years to come. You may get the opportunity to evolve back to your industry as an expert in your field now working for yourself as a consultant. Who knows? Your best and most profitable professional years may be in the years to come. Which raises another issue: What about the conflict of retirement?

Instead of retiring, we should be graduating!

As I've said, I am opposed to the American concept of retirement. Voluntary death is a closely related concept. Do you know someone who retired from professional life and then physically died soon after? The truth is, the last chapter of our lives should be our best. Instead of retiring, we should be graduating! About the time we have finally experienced life enough to know something, we begin to talk about quitting. We should not avoid the conflict of aging, but welcome it by making choices that will allow us to be purposefully active every day that we live.

Placing our complete confidence in whatever it is that we think we know today may be the worst mistake we could ever make.

Change through the impact of technology is also creating conflict in our professional lives. What we know today may be irrelevant to what we need to know tomorrow. The life of software and hardware in today's rapid-fire digital age is getting shorter and shorter. Placing our complete confidence in whatever it is that we think we know today may be the worst mistake we could ever make. Life must be seen for what it is. It is a perpetual learning experience. Instead of resisting it, we must "go to school" every single day of our lives. You must choose to step out of whatever rut you might be in and stay humble enough to learn something new. That brings us to a perspective discussion that is foundational to embracing conflict: the issue of rightness.

Where and when does it become valuable for you to declare yourself to be right about anything? Life is not about our being right: It's about being open to unique discovery every day. It's about staying humble enough to remember in every situation that there may be something there for us to learn. The declaration and insistence upon rightness will always set the stage for judgment, disrespect, and division, a serious abuse of the power found in conflict. Today, like never before, must be about learning. I am not suggesting that we shouldn't passionately hold our convictions. I've already established the importance of conviction in living life on purpose. This is an issue of disposition that must undergird conviction. Conviction that refuses to be filtered through the spirit of humility and openness is bound to become abuse.

When you see conflict for what it is, you see opportunity. You see the potential for learning something new. You see the potential for doing new things in new ways that might revolutionize life as you know it, and that might not be all bad. You recognize the need for patience, both for yourself and for the people in your world, as we face tough choices. No longer does change take on an appearance that has to be feared. But at the same time, it must be respected for what it represents: the next great step to the rest of your life.

PERFORMANCE: ANTICIPATION AND PREPARATION

Because life is about choices, we face conflict daily. Change is inevitable—it's just a matter of how, when, and where. Hiding will not work. Denial is wasted time. Avoidance is a failed strategy. The answer lies in anticipation. Sharpen your skills of anticipating your daily conflict. Go back to the "chicken people" illustration in chaper 6. Think back about the power of anticipation as it was introduced in the previous chapter on making the communication connection.

How often have you caught yourself tripping over the same conflicts day after day? In the words of my grandson, Caleb, "How does that make sense?" Years ago while working for a division of Johnson and Johnson, I was first introduced to the power of this life strategy. Through our sales training, we were taught to anticipate and prepare for any customer situation we might encounter. We were trained how to anticipate customer objections and script positive responses that would produce results. One little drill we did had to do with facing the worst. How do you handle a customer confrontation that is getting out of control? I remember thinking to myself that this training was probably overkill. But we practiced for it nevertheless.

Then I was transferred to Northern California where I had the "tough" job of traveling down scenic Highway 1 from the Bay Area on the north to Carmel on the south. It was a tough life but somebody had to do it. I also had territorial responsibilities that took me east across the mountains to the Fresno area. Because I was so enamored with the coast, I didn't make it out east in my first few months. One day I received a call from my home office telling me that I had to get out to one of the hospitals in Fresno. They were angry and were about to destroy a piece of equipment we had placed in the hospital—and the cost would be enormous. Charged with the responsibility of turning the situation around, I first had to find out how to get to Fresno. I then drove late into the night and was at the hospital by 8:00 A.M. the next morning. The person in charge of central supply told me rather rudely to take a seat. I followed her directions and I waited. In just a matter of minutes, four very angry women joined the already angry person I was with and they all gathered in a semicircle around me. Looking down upon me in my chair with my little briefcase by my side, they proceeded to vent. At that point in my life I was familiar with profanity, but I must say, these ladies took it to a whole new level. I couldn't believe it. I was in the middle of the very thing we had anticipated and prepared for during our training. Almost instinctively, I began to respond to them as I had been trained: First, I singled one of them out and began to smile. Her response was just as I had been taught it would be. She stopped the tirade and looked at me and said, "Are you just going to sit there with that stupid smile on your face?" I was so blown away by the accuracy of the anticipation in our training that I almost forgot where to go from there. I began by affirming them in their anger. I told them that everything they had said, except that part about my mother, had been true. We did not deserve their business, based on our performance, and I would remove the equipment from the hospital. I then ask them if they would like to see how it was supposed to have worked. They said yes, and I suddenly was on the road to creating a new relationship with what became a great customer.

What is the point of that story? Is it just how great a salesman I was? Absolutely not! I have messed up more of those opportunities than I have handled. The point is, because of anticipation I was prepared. I have worked with customer service departments across a wide range of businesses, and the situation is all too often the same. Some of the most frustrated people in the world are on the telephone or face to face daily with the very people you need in order to be successful. The reason for their frustration lies in their lack of preparation to deal with the conflicts they will inevitably encounter. When people are not prepared, they will not be confident. And when people are not confident, they will be reactive. The answer is to anticipate and prepare. Create scripts that have been purposed. Then, practice those scripts until you have confidently made them your own.

This same principle applies for all of your life. Just think what a difference you would feel in your life if you took the time to anticipate and prepare for the day ahead. I typically get up early enough to let exercise jumpstart my day. It's important to exercise both my mind and my body, so when I am on my game I will take the time during those sessions to reflect upon my upcoming day. I do that prayerfully first. I then do that practically and visually. I try to visualize the people I will meet and the places I will be today. Instead of just running into my schedule, I want to anticipate and prepare for the events on my schedule. Obviously that begins with my family. I have to get my mind straight about my interaction with them, especially in the morning, or I am going to crash before I ever get started. When I discipline myself to take this time to launch my day I am always blessed and I also believe I am more effective.

Do yourself a favor and get prepared for the life you know you will live. I certainly am not suggesting that you can anticipate everything that will happen in your life because that's impossible. I do believe, however, that with practice we can learn to anticipate and prepare for 90 percent-plus of all that will happen. Think what a difference that could make!

MAKING CONFLICT WORK FOR YOU

Purposed living all begins with a mindset that conflict with its choices and changes can produce powerful and positive results. It includes a vision of every day through passionate and humble eyes that see potential for learning and growing. And it involves making the preparation necessary to put it all into motion.

Because conflict is a force, it must be handled with care; it must be purposed. You can avoid it for a while. You can pretend that it is not there; you can deny its presence. But it's there all the same. This powerful resource with its potential for creative development is just waiting for your leadership. It's only a matter of what level of leadership you will provide. Without your leadership, the conflict will be left to chance, and what are the odds that the outcome will be positive?

TAKE THE CHALLENGE

Pursue the following simple leadership strategy for the next thirty days. Embrace the process and celebrate the results.

1. *Begin tomorrow by allowing yourself time to visualize your day.* See yourself in the places and with the people you have before you. Think about the outcome you hope to achieve in each one and prepare your mind for them.
2. *If you manage people, meet with them and help them anticipate the challenges they have before them.* Using the communication pattern you learned in the last chapter let them prethink and create scripts that will best serve the needs of the company, their customers, and their own personal confidence.
3. *Practice and perform professionally.* We all work from scripts. Too often what we say day in and day out is not reflective of responsive professionalism. By purposefully creating scripts and by practicing them until we have internalized them as our own, we will more confidently impact the people we are seeking to influence.

Let these suggestions help you personally and corporately live a purposed tomorrow. Remember, you choose. Victim or leader?

AFFIRMATIONS

I will embrace conflict confidently.
I will choose to face the changes I must make.
I will see each day and each conflict as opportunity.
I will anticipate the challenges I will face.
I will use conflict as my resource.
I will not let conflict make me its victim.

THE
SELLING
LIFESTYLE

In working with various professionals across the country, I have learned that one way to grab their attention from the very beginning is to tell them that they are all salesmen. How do you think they react to being identified as salesmen? They resent it. They immediately resist it. But through further discussion, it becomes obvious that the thing they resist is their perception of what it means to be in selling.

In one particular organization, being totally brain dead to the negative perception selling carries for most people, I presented "selling" as an important culture theme. The reaction was swift and sure. The problem, however, was not with the audience, but with me as a coach. Instead of beginning with them and their reality, I began with me and mine. While I'm convinced we are all involved in selling on a daily basis, I have learned to accept the unfortunate image it represents in the minds of most.

In this chapter, as with each of the preceding chapters, we will begin with what you think about selling. With renewed conviction, we will reflect upon its image. Then we will focus upon the life application of it all. As a side note, I will be specifically providing insight for selling professionals.

In the minds of most people, selling is synonymous with manipulation and dishonesty. The picture most often brought to mind is a sleazy, used-car salesperson. I hasten to say that many in used-car selling have become victims of overgeneralization. Unfortunately, because so many in their field deal abusively with the public, all of them get the backlash. The truth is, every field has those who misrepresent professionalism to the public. It certainly is not limited to the used-car business.

In the minds of most people, selling is synonymous with manipulation and dishonesty.

Some of the people who most resist this universal sales idea are involved in some of our most prestigious professions. When I tell physicians, dentists, lawyers, accountants, teachers, and other like professionals that they are in sales, their backs bow quickly. I believe that this problem stems from an insufficient understanding of the difference between a professional ideal and business reality. Physicians and dentists go through an intense education devoted almost entirely to the clinical skills of their profession. There is no argument that the focus on this dimension is vital. No one wants to hire a surgeon who made a C in anatomy! For the law student, it is essential to be equipped with the technical rules of law. The accountant must master the minutia of tax and financial planning. It's a given that each of these professionals must become skilled masters of their chosen technologies. But professionals, no matter how skilled, who can't relate to people are just as unprepared for operating a practice as those who failed to receive proper technical training. They'd be like million-dollar homes built on a foundation for a double-wide trailer.

Years ago during my mortgage banking years, my company was asked to provide financing for a prestigious subdivision developing in our area. We were excited about what this higher-dollar lending meant for our company, but unfortunately we had not anticipated what was really involved in this "great opportunity." The houses were built, loans were made, and people proudly moved into their new homes. Then the shifts began. The houses had been built upon shifting ground, and none of the foundations had been laid with that possibility in mind.

Piers should have been driven deeply into the ground to anchor these homes, but they were not. These beautiful and elabo-rate constructions began to come apart. Cracks widened. Homeowners were furious and quickly sought legal remedy. We went suddenly from delight to disgust. Great excitement quickly turned to finan-cial exposure and loss. In so many cases, the greatest distractions in our lives come disguised as opportunity.

In so many cases, the greatest distractions in our lives come disguised as opportunity.

Please hear me say that there must be a professional foundation to your success. But beyond that, you face the daily challenge of selling what you know. It not only applies to business, it applies to husbands, wives, parents, friends, church members, service organizations, and children as well. You are selling something every day: You are either selling your services, your products, your-self, or what you believe to be true.

PHILOSOPHY: INFLUENCE AND CHOICE

Selling has gotten a bad wrap. What it represents is not what it is at all. Actually, selling is closely related to leadership. Here is a definition that I have embraced for most of my professional life: Selling is the way you influence the minds of others in an attempt to help them choose. *Professional* selling is influencing the minds of others in such a way as to help them choose and, in the process, to help you prosper. It does not require manipulation. It does not involve convincing or pushing. In its basic nature, it does not even involve convincing anyone of any-thing.

Respect

Perhaps the most significant element to a healthy and proper understanding of the selling lifestyle is respect. Every human being must be respected for who they are as a unique and purposed creation of God. They have both the right and the responsibility to choose for themselves in this life. Any relationship that majors in one individual choosing for another is unhealthy and will ultimately suffer. On the other hand, we do have a mutual challenge in this life to choose, creating the essence of conflict. With that in mind, you have the daily opportunity to help people with their burden of conflict. Your personal selling role is to provide them the benefit of both what you know and what you may have experienced.

The problem seems to come when our conviction becomes a mandate for others or when our personal need supercedes the respect we have for our fellow human beings. When either of these conditions exists, pressure will be applied. When we believe what we believe so strongly that we want everybody to own it with us, we are standing on pivotal ground. Expressing that conviction with passion and with personal concern is a vital part of the human experience. Insisting, however, that your conviction must become the conviction of another crosses the line of respect.

We face the challenge to model our respect for others every day. Some of those challenges are simple, while others can be the ultimate challenge to relationship. The abortion question in this country provides great evidence for conviction that insists on expression and, unfortunately, conviction that too often crosses the line to abuse. Any woman who faces the spiritual, emotional, physical, and social dilemma of an unwanted pregnancy deserves and needs the support of people in her world. She needs people who will help her examine her options.

If I were trying to influence her, I would do all that I could to help her know that there is hope and help for tomorrow. I would encourage her to see that by having her baby she would be bringing new potential to this world. I would encourage her to understand that she can receive help and support for raising her child, and I would help her find it. I would help her know that if she does not believe that she can raise and support her child that there are couples who are praying now for a child and the opportunity to play that parenting role for her.

They would even let her play whatever part they mutually believe would be best for the child. I would plead with her not to abort the child, which would be making a choice that only God is qualified to make. But I also would be there to drive her home from the abortion clinic, if that was her choice. I would be there to provide the care that she would need for healing spiritually, emotionally, physically, and socially. I would not agree with her choice, but I would be there to help her make new choices for her tomorrow.

Just a side note for all who might read this and think that I am overlooking the rights and feelings of the unborn: I have strong conviction that the yet-to-be-born who tragically have their birth terminated are receiving all of the care that they require from the Father of life. They are, no doubt, the most blessed. They live, yet they never have to experience the pain, confusion, and insecurity of this life. Who really is the victim in an abortion? I am personally convicted that it is not the unborn. It's the mother and father who have to live in the consequences of that judgment. I must respect, however, the conviction you have or the choice you make in that regard.

While we may have something as serious as abortion to discuss on one side, we also find ourselves in the same selling role every day in obviously much less impacting arenas of discussion, like where we will choose to eat tonight or where we will go on vacation, or what kind of car we will buy, or what college our child will attend. You will, no doubt, have feelings about each and every one of these life situations. The question is: How successful are you in influencing functional and harmonious choices?

Knowledge

What does all of this have to do with selling? Everything! Selling cuts across every dimension of your life. With its great depth and far-reaching effect, selling is at the heart of relationship building. The essence of productivity is the influence we have upon one another. And I believe it needs to be the *purposed* influence we have upon others. If so, along with respect for others must come knowledge and insight. We owe it to each other to continue to learn and grow every day. I need to do it both for you and for me. After all, how can I provide you the insight you might need to make choices if I know nothing about what you are facing?

Several years ago, I had a learning opportunity come my way in a most unexpected package. Barbara let me know that we were invited to a family reunion for folks on her mother's side of the family. Now I have to let you in on something about me that I don't regard as a personal strength. On a "gag me" meter from one to ten, family reunions are about an eight for me. It says more about me than it does about my family, nevertheless that is how it is and Barbara knows it. So it should go without saying that I was not excited about this familial event. In her sweet way, Barbara explained to me how it would be in my best interest to attend, and so we did. I may not be too smart, but I am no fool.

As I was standing at the back of the room watching the reunion unfold around me, I could not help but notice a group of people standing around a very old man. I asked Barb's mom about the man getting all of the attention, and she told me he was Uncle Claude, who'd just turned 100 years old. I had never met a person that old. I watched as he feebly got up and walked across the room without help. I could not believe it. I don't know what I expected, but I know I did not expect what I got. I waited my turn. Then I met Claude and spent the rest of the afternoon in one of the most intriguing and insightful conversations of my life. Born before the turn of the twentieth century, he told me so many incredible things about the Depression, the war years, and about the enormous advances in communication and transportation. Yet it was his contemporariness that got my attention. He was more up to date on world events than I am, and I think I stay pretty well informed. And his life insight on almost every level held me spellbound. I later learned that Claude read every day of his life and had been a leader in the early days of the Texas library movement. Reading was his passion and, as a result, he could discuss intelligently almost any subject. Claude had purposely prepared his whole life to provide positive influence, and he was most successful!

Here is the point. Selling requires your knowledge of something. If you are going to be able to provide any kind of purposed support or influence on those around you, you must read something. Everywhere I speak, I talk to people about reading. The most common reaction I get from folks is that they just don't read. "I am just not into reading," they will say. "Well, are you into eating?" is my typical response. I don't say it to be cute. I believe it is just that significant to your role in the twenty-first century. If you're looking for something good to read, I've included a booklist for you at the back of this book. You can also keep up with my updated book recommendations on my Web site, www.TappeGroup.com. Please give reading a try. It will change your life. And it will put you in better position to influence the lives around you.

Conviction

Whereas respect is foundational to a proper understanding about selling, and knowledge is basic to your sphere of influence, without conviction, very little selling will ever get done. I have already said quite a bit about conviction, but most of it was on the side of abuse. I believe one of the tragically missing ingredients in our world today is conviction. Tolerance for others out of respect for them as fellow human beings does not mean I have to forfeit my right to passionate conviction. You have every right to be convicted about what you believe. I believe it is totally appropriate for us to be confident that where we stand is the right place to be. The more strongly I believe, the more obvious it should become through my life and through my words. My conviction, however, should never invade the life of another person unless I have lost sight of my fundamental commitment to mutual respect or unless consequences for their choices coincide with my own personal convictions (such as any punishment as a consequence for breaking the law).

With a philosophical foundation that embraces selling as a lifestyle, things change. We begin to see life differently. Our world takes on a new and much more purposed view.

PERSPECTIVE: NEED AND AWARENESS

One of the foundational principles in professional selling is the discipline of prospecting. I will have much more to say about this specific discipline in the "Performance" section that follows, where I will speak directly to selling professionals. At this juncture, I raise the issue to make a specific point. The effectiveness of my life is directly proportional to my connection to the people around me. In other words, if I look at life as though I am the only reason for living, then life can get pretty dark. On the other hand, if I live life every day as though I have something to "sell" in my world, then each day takes on new clarity.

Yourself

The place to find perspective in selling begins with your product. What are you selling in life? Here is an important question for you to consider: Who is the person who influences you most? Think about it. I would be surprised if you

The most influential person in your life is yourself.

were to get this one right. The answer is so obvious yet so hard to recognize. The most influential person in your life is yourself. You have more influence upon you than anyone else in the world. No one spends more time with you than you. No one has more to say to you than you. So are you having the kind of influence upon yourself that you want to? What are you selling yourself? Are you selling yourself the things that will serve to make life better, or worse? Most people are their own worst enemy. The first place to begin exercising your power as a selling professional is on yourself. Once you have sold yourself on you and upon your reason for living, then you will have no problem selling others.

Spouse

What kind of influence do you want to have on the people around you? Do you believe in your influence strongly enough to make it a purposed contribution in the lives of those in your world? Begin with those you love most. If you are married, it becomes increasingly important to sell your partner on your love each and every day. This is very different from the story of the older couple who went to the counselor with marriage trouble. The wife complained that her husband never told her that he loved her. When questioned by the counselor, the man said, "I told her thirty years ago that I loved her, and if that ever changes I will let her know." This is not a great selling approach to marriage. The longer you're married, the more important it is to remind each other of your committed love. I am constantly amazed by men who just do not understand how essential it is for them to continue to creatively reaffirm their love for the woman in their life.

Children

Parenting requires a continual process of selling to your children in a variety of different ways. From the very beginning much of your work is nonverbal. Children must be reassured of your love through your touch. Hugging becomes an important selling gesture for us as parents who want our children to grow up with the confidence of our love. They need to feel our nurturing. That need never goes away. My girls are grown and pretty much on their own, but I am more aware now of their need for my touch than ever before. Trust is a relationship that you would hope your children would learn and enjoy as part of your family. It is also an experience you hope they will enjoy as a product of building their own. If that is the case, then it is vital for you to model that relationship for them through your marriage, as a parent, as a son or daughter, as a friend, as a church member, and through any other relationship you might be attempting to build.

Friends

Friendship is such an easy word to say. I have been in more than one circumstance where the relationship of acquaintance and friendship was being confused. I have been introduced to audiences as a good friend to the one providing the introduction when in reality we are acquaintances at best. Friendships are built through mutually committed and invested time. Friends don't wait for friends to call. Friends call first. Real wealth in this life is not found in bank accounts. Rather, it will be found in the relationships that have been forged in this life. Friendships do not just happen. They have to be built on purpose.

Your World

What kind of influence are you choosing to have upon your world? The world is being sold something by you on a daily basis. How do you approach your life as a professional? Do you believe you can make a real difference upon the company you work for? Because you probably spend more than half of your waking life in some professional environment, that has an incredible impact upon the rest of your life. To create a positive working culture, choose to see

Every day and every person you meet provide you selling opportunities.

each day as an opportunity to encourage your fellow workers. You are capable of having an incredible influence upon the lives of those around you. It has to be a sell you believe in, and it must be done on purpose.

In your community, in your service club, in your professional organizations, and in your church, selling is going on. You are having an influence. But before you can have a powerful and purposed influence, you have to see possibility: Every day and every person you meet provide you selling opportunities. Many choices you face each day can become more manageable once you choose the personal product you intend to sell. Just yesterday, for instance, I was invited to join a local community service organization. Though it is a great organization and one that I personally respect for the generous contribution it makes, I turned down the invitation because I knew that *now* is not the time for me to make any new commitments. I do not believe in belonging for appearance sake. Whether it is Rotary or church, I believe membership demands commitment and contribution. It is a very real part of the life I am trying to sell to my world. So, to join and not contribute would be a personal contradiction. I would not be representing my own product with integrity.

It would be important for you to take a good look at your life "sales terri-tory." Think about the personal conviction package you represent to your world. Selling is happening. You are influencing the thinking in your world. Do you see it? Do you recognize the influence you could have?

PERFORMANCE: PERSISTENCE AND MOMENTUM

Selling is really a science—it's a numbers game. It is a pursuit requiring persist-ence and results in momentum. For those who pursue selling as a professional career, making contacts on a regular and consistent basis is a prerequisite to suc-cess. The contacts you make today will dictate the success you will enjoy tomor-row. If contacts are not made on purpose, you will be out of business. While these comments are specifically intended for selling professionals, the application of the principle is intended for all of us. The purposed personal contacts you make today will determine the quality of the personal life you will enjoy tomorrow.

So what kind of influence do you intend to sell to your world today? As a pur-posed performer, each day must be approached with great anticipation, planning, and purpose. I believe the place to begin is with you. You need to sell yourself on the value and responsibility found in each day before you actually live it.

> *The contacts you make today will dictate the success you will enjoy tomorrow.*

I personally believe the starting point must be with you and God. Prayer and meditation lift you into an entirely new dimension to begin your day, and I highly recommend including music. Listening to music that praises God, complemented by time of relation-ship with him, puts life into the powerful perspective you need to perform pur-posefully. It reminds you that you are not alone: You have a personal Power well beyond you who is working in your day. It lifts your spirit to know that you will somehow be used in this divine show.

Over and over again, I am amazed at the powerful Presence of God. Recently

I had an experience that proves it. I got to my speaking engagement a little early, and I had the opportunity to meet a young woman who was the first person in the room. She came right up to the front of this large room and took a seat on one of the first few rows. I met her and commended her for her punctuality and for her choice in seating. She laughed and suggested that she probably deserved a prize for being the first to arrive. I quickly agreed and went to my briefcase where I found a copy of Bruce Wilkinson's little book, *The Prayer of Jabez*. When I gave it to her she responded somewhat emotionally in disbelief. She said that a woman earlier that day had told her that she needed to get a copy of that book. She was so grateful. I later learned that this young woman was going through a very difficult time in her marriage. She said that the affirmation of God's Presence to her through my giving her that book meant more than I could ever know. What if you began every day of your life knowing that you would be used by God that day in some very purposed way?

Take a moment and "mind" through your day. Who will you meet? What do you know you can expect? Begin with your family. Purpose to bring a positive message to them from your very first word. Don't wait for them to start with you. So often, I let my day get out of control from the very beginning by letting it happen to me before I am ready. When I can begin by saying the things to Barbara that I want to say before the insanity of the day begins, things just get off to a better start for us both. Selling-contact needs to be made with the people in my life if I ever intend to influence them with purpose and with power. The same is true for my children. In fact, I believe in spending the morning making sure that all the people I regard as being on my life team receive my attention. Like prospecting in professional selling, making contact with my life team is always best to do first, before the day begins to mess with me. Spend time each morning making those important personal contacts, and your life will improve. I guarantee it!

As you move quickly from the people dimension of your life into the professional, you move onto a stage that requires professional discipline and accountability. It doesn't really matter how things are going for you personally or even physically. When you step onto your professional stage, you make a statement. The question is, do you present the message you intend? Are you making the difference you have purposed to make? In order for that to be the case, we can't allow personal things to influence our professional life; we can't react to some injustice or insanity we recognize in our colleagues or in our company; we can't allow our position to dictate our purpose. Remember you choose. When you allow forces outside of you to determine your course of action, no matter what they might be, you become a victim, and you probably will victimize others in the process. In the personal-selling context, you are responsible for both product and presentation. There are no excuses because you are the only one they can be made to.

I remember having a vision of just how ridiculous it is for people to make excuses for their life performance. My family loves the theater, so when *Phantom of the Opera* came to Dallas it was almost a foregone conclusion we would go. Only one of my daughters had seen this musical classic, and so I secured tickets for all of us. They were pumped. On the day of the performance, I had been working with an organization filled with people challenges. People were not getting along with one another. Morale was low. Production was down. Profits were unacceptable. As I took my seat alongside Barbara and the girls that evening, this company drama was on my mind. Just before the curtain went up, I had this vision:

I imagined a cast member coming onto the stage to say a few words just before the play began. After welcoming us warmly, I imagined him giving us some necessary disclosures. With some sense of apology, he warned us that there was some role confusion and conflict in the cast. Hopefully, they would work through them and it wouldn't prove to be a factor in the performance. He went on to let us know that some cast members were having some personal and marriage conflicts: Some were recovering from a particularly difficult day with the children; some were from dysfunctional backgrounds and families. Some of them were dealing with allergy-related problems, while others were struggling with hormonal issues. On behalf of everyone in the cast, he just wanted us to know what they were up against and for us to do our best to enjoy the evening.

I realize that this was just my imagination, but if it did happen what would you think? Would it be out of line in that context for me not to care? For me, that would be way too much information. You would expect more from professionals. They took your money, and you would be well within your rights to expect a professional performance no matter what. And that is the point. In the professional dimension of our lives, particularly, we need to be our best. We need to make sure we are delivering the message we intend to deliver, both personally and professionally.

Your performance each day is an expression of what you believe, so it needs to be purposed and powerful. Make sure you are representing the life product you intend to be selling. Make sure your intentions and your performance stay in harmony.

SELLING LIFE ON PURPOSE

I hope you will not be offended by your new designation as a life salesperson. You sell life daily. You influence people in your world. How you choose to make that happen is now up to you. I encourage you to accept this new designation with purpose and commitment.

Not only must you know your product, you have to believe strongly in it because there is no question that your degree of passion for what you sell greatly impacts any success you might hope to achieve. Whether it is a tangible product or an intangible service that you sell, it all begins with your reason *why*. It certainly will involve your sense of significance in the process, your *what*. And, it will receive its energy from the determination you have toward reaching your destination, your *where*. Remember, motivation is the issue.

Once you accept the fact that you are selling a product, everyday life changes.

You no longer see life as something to be endured but something to produce. You can no longer simply take the position of consumer.

Now, you have work to do. You have a reason to live. You have a cause to pursue. You have a new sell to make every day. Life may be difficult, but it is also an exciting privilege.

TAKE THE CHALLENGE

Here are some steps I would encourage you to take immediately.

1. *Internalize your product.* You have to believe in what you sell. For that to happen, you must be thoroughly familiar with it. Spend some time getting in touch with what kind of influence you intend to have upon your world. Discover how much passion you have for who you are in life. Think about what it is you do and why you do it. Stay in touch with your own purpose and mission statements. Read them and repeat them often to yourself over the course of the next thirty days.

2. *Identify your market.* Target the significant players in your world. Once that is done, think about how effectively you make contact with this significant part of your world every day. Don't be surprised to discover that you spend a great deal of time with people who do not appear on your list. You may need to make some changes.

3. *Intensify your contacts.* You influence people every day, so commit to make that influence on purpose. Examine not only the time you spend with the essential people in your world, but also the quality of your contacts. Presentation is everything in selling. So think about the kind of presentational changes you may need to make as a husband, wife, parent, child, employee, citizen, and friend. Don't wait. Make them.

AFFIRMATIONS

I will sell my world with purpose and conviction.

I will provide the opportunity for people to choose.

I will respect the choices of the people in my world.

I will identify and consistently contact the significant people in my world.

I will always look for opportunity to improve my life presentation.

I have reason to live today.

THE REALITY
OF TEAM

Team may be one of the most abused four-letter words in our vocabulary. Somehow, it became a '90s thing to refer to everything as team. Committees suddenly became teams. Everyone from McDonalds to financial organizations adopted the idea of team. A few banks even incorporated the term "team" into their names as they reorganized and remarketed themselves to the world. Many have begun to look to professional athletic coaches as the gurus who can give them a competitive edge. And some of these coaches have made great contributions to the understanding of our world. John Wooden, the legendary UCLA basketball coach, is an example of a man who has used his insight with athletes to help many of us understand life a little better. In reality, it was his understanding of life that made him such a great coach.

We have discussed the power of people. Team is how we work together *with* people. Team is an easy and even winning expression to use, but it is a lot harder to do. The functional choices that must be made to be a team presents unique challenges. Because team has both relational and functional implications, the two often get confused. In other words, you don't have a choice about being a member of the "human team," but you do have choices about how you function within the team.

Our most obvious and important choice involves identifying team on a personal level. This puzzle piece is the most challenging because it involves both choosing and being chosen. Whether you are a manager seeking an employee or a young person seeking a spouse, the person you choose may determine your future quality of life. I can't emphasize enough how important it is for you to choose carefully and consistently, using your values as a filter. That obviously means you must first clarify to yourself both your personal as well as your corporate values. Most employee problems are hired problems. Most marriage problems happen because of a lack of agreement about, or commitment to, a mutual sense of authority.

Many have lost sight of the most significant gift we have in this life: our intertwined interdependency.

No one flies solo. It even took a team of three to bring you into this world—man, woman, and God—and you never cease to be involved in this team sport called life. As I have said, many have confused organizational strategy with relational reality. Just because your company has chosen to let you work on your own doesn't mean that you somehow cease to need and depend upon the people in the world around you. Being single, relationally speaking, doesn't mean that you somehow cease to have responsibility and relationship within the human family. Many have lost sight of the most significant gift we have in this life: our intertwined interdependency. Confusion and frustration too often reign because of misunderstanding about this thing called team.

I once had a call from a man who identified himself as a team leader for his company. He said that as a group they had a certain number of hours of team training they had to provide and attend each year and that I had come highly recommended. He then proceeded to tell me how dismal their experience had been with team training. In fact, he told me that in the previous year they had set up two days of training with an organization and after the first day they had terminated the relationship. Things just weren't working out.

After he had clarified the challenge to me, I thanked him for the call and then told him that I really didn't think I would be his best choice. In response to his inquiry as to why, I told him that I really believed I would quickly become his worst nightmare. I went on to explain that from the brief insights he had shared, it was clear to me that he didn't believe in team. In fact, it seemed that he probably resented the whole exercise as being an inconvenience and irrelevant. I explained that in the first few moments of our training I would say things that would, no doubt, expose him as being a team leader who didn't believe in team. For that reason, I told him that it would probably be best for him to choose someone more closely aligned with him in philosophy. After a long pause, he then said, "I think you may be just what we need." We spent a whole day debating and defining team for this group of professionals. It turned out to be an enlightening experience for us all.

Some confuse their natural inclinations toward independence or even their behavioral tendencies as reality. Remember, just because you feel a given way doesn't make it that way. However, until you change the way you think, you will always see life through the eyes of independence and self-centeredness. And of course, if that is the way you see life, your performance will conform to your self-imposed vision, and team will always be a great frustration for you. Please consider the following progression.

Philosophy: Reality and Relationship

Team is your reality. You have no choice about it. But how you decide to play your role in response to those around you is your choice. In fact, you are the only one who can really make it. No matter what relationship you are considering, you are the only one who can choose how you will live it. By definition, I believe that team includes and involves anyone you depend upon for your success.

Choice is the beginning point for any real understanding about team. With the significant exceptions of your creation and your family of origin, you always have choice about the teams you will join in life. It is important to say at this point that even when your draw in life seems unfair with regard to your family or to your family of origin, you do not have to be a victim unless you choose to be one. Recall my comments about Dave Pelzer and draw strength from his story. He, like so many others I have met, have taken amazing childhood and family obstacles and turned them into a life-fitness program. These people have gone on in life to become incredible influences for good. They refused to be held back by the seemingly limiting and abusive factors surrounding their birth. Unfortunately, I have met more people who have made a life out of blaming their circumstances for the choices they ultimately have made.

The same is true in corporate life. Too many employees blame their employers for their choice of career or employment. At the same time, too many managers and owners spend far too much time blaming employees for the hiring choices they have made. Team needs to begin with agreement. In fact, basic agreements need to characterize all of your teaming efforts. Today, I believe our biggest challenges relate to what I will refer to as "virtual teaming." It isn't just the people on my team of choice; it's all the people I "inherit" as a result of my pursuit. In marriage, it relates to in-laws. In parenting, it relates to schools, teachers, and our children's friends. In companies, it revolves around customers, vendors, and projects. For any team to function with any degree of success, some agreement must be reached. On a recent flight to Vancouver, Washington, I was seated next to a young businessman who was born and raised in the Republic of South Africa. Having lived in that country myself, we spent time discussing the triumphs and the tragedies of South Africa. One thing is for sure, few people understand the scope of the challenge in that small country at the tip of the African continent. The challenge there revolves around the issue of foundational agreement: People cannot substantively agree upon how they will live together. Tribal allegiance reigns above team recognition and cooperation. A solution seems impossible. Unless, and until, some basic agreement is reached, the country will continue to live in conflict and turmoil.

Agreement of Values

The place to begin is with agreement about expectations. What can we expect from one another? Anytime there is disagreement and division among people, you can always know that it is an expectation problem. Unfortunately, most often expectations have never been discussed, much less agreed upon. Expectations involve not just the *what* of the matter but more importantly the *how*. The most significant agreement to be reached with regard to expectations involves values. It is a major mistake in any relationship to assume that just because you believe in something or about something that other people will be in automatic agreement.

Trust

One particular value that must exist in order for any positive team result to occur is trust. *Trust* is a most misunderstood word. Too many people see trust as something that people just do. You might have someone say, "You will just have to trust me about this." Trust is not something you do. Trust is a relationship that is developed through the mutually shared experience of honesty and integrity.

Be careful about making assumptions about honesty. I have yet to meet a person or group of people who would suggest that dishonesty is a good basis from which to work. It goes without saying, honesty should exist between us, but unfortunately, the problem begins with "it goes without saying." Your understanding and conviction about honesty may be quite different from the world around you. I'll never forget a conversation I had with a colleague who told me that he believed honesty related only to the things he said, not the things he did not say, even if they were implied. What he called honesty, I called deception. While my conviction did not make me any better than him as a human being, it did make me more effective as a team player, because he could never be trusted. I have also found being honest is much easier said than done. People with great conviction about honesty will compromise that conviction in the face of conflict. Because of personal discomfort or pressure, honesty can get lost. Think of a time when you found yourself not being honest because of your desire to fit in or please another person. I believe it is a challenge we all face, and it needs to be talked about at the beginning of any team relationship. You need to give the people on your life teams permission to be honest with you, and then you need to make it easy for them when they do.

Integrity

Integrity is the testimony of honesty. Integrity means that you will do what you say you will. Once again, integrity, like honesty, is like Mom and apple pie. Everyone is for it, yet living it is a challenge for us all. I think one of the most obvious integrity issues facing professionals in the twenty-first century involves keeping schedules and being on time. It is the height of arrogance for a person to make an appointment with someone and then to have total disregard for keeping the commitment. Many physicians seem to believe they have a corner on the market for importance in commitments to time. Countless times I have been made to wait to see a doctor. A sign in one doctor's office says, "We value promptness. If you are late fifteen minutes for your appointment, you will be rescheduled." That sounds reasonable. The problem is, patients often are forced to wait over an hour to see that doctor! It's clear that the patient's time is not valued! What makes the doctor's time more valuable than mine? To be told that they are running late because they had an emergency is a catchall, overused copout. Let me see blood or hear a "code blue." I believe it is closer to the truth that the doctor and his team are totally out of sync, and they don't regard seeing patients on time as a matter of integrity. You can't help but wonder what else you won't be able to trust them about. It should go without saying that this is not just a physician problem.

I will never forget a lesson my youngest daughter taught me about integrity. Trying to treat each of my young daughters as unique individuals, I committed to having a "dad time" with them individually each week. One morning, Barbara caught Meredith, at age seven, going through my briefcase, and she asked her what she was doing. Meredith said that she was looking for my book. After further inquiry, Barbara was able to deduce that Meredith was looking for my appointment book to see if her name was there for that week. She had learned early that if her name was in my book she had a chance of fitting into my schedule. If her name was not in my book, there was not much of a chance that she would get her time with me. She wanted to know if she was a priority in my life. She wanted to know if she could trust me to keep my word. Thankfully, she found her name there. At age seven, she was questioning my integrity, and she didn't even know it.

We will never be perfect. We will all miss appointments and run late from time to time. But because team is built on mutual trust, those times need to be the exception, not the rule. Teams have to reach agreement about the nonnegotiables—the base to which they can always return. Most of the teams I have worked with seem to come up with a similar list of values: Trust, honesty, and integrity are always there. Respect is always near the top of the list.

Many times commitment and loyalty are included. Interestingly enough, kindness and compassion are becoming a major part of the discussion. It is not at all unusual to hear forgiveness promoted. Communication and recognition are also often included. The key is to engage the team in the process. Once values are in place, culture can be built. Until mutual agreement is reached and team commitment is made, everyone will be right in their own eyes.

Team will always require some degree of sacrifice. You cannot have it all your way. If everything has to come your way then you are not being team, you are simply trying to be multiples of yourself. When a group of individuals come together and commit to mutually defined and shared values and behavioral standards, life changes. You become an active participant in a creative process that has power and possibility that goes well beyond what can be produced by any individual or group of people insisting upon living independent of one another.

PERSPECTIVE: CONFIDENCE AND SECURITY

Without the reality of team, life would be missing several key ingredients that only relationship can ultimately provide. The most significant relationship in life is the relationship we have with our Creator. As I have said, what you do with relationship is a matter of personal choice, and that choice produces important implications. Besides personal motivation, the issues of security, identity, and purpose are ultimately spiritual questions. You are the one who chooses. My only suggestion would be that your choices measure up to the relationship needs that are basic to your life.

We are living in a world where many claim that technology can fill the relational gaps of life, but I disagree. Neither computers, robotics, nor virtual experiences will ever be able to meet the relational needs that we all have deep within us. Without spiritual centering we will be overwhelmed by twenty-first century challenges. And time spent in Internet chat rooms can't replace the positive relationships with people in your life. I need people who are willing to play roles of support and protection for me. Without them, my back will always go uncovered. I need people behind me for protection and beside me for companionship. Life would be empty and sad without the presence of the people I care for and who I know care for me. Without question, I need people who go before me to provide leadership. People who are willing to step out in life as pioneers play a sacrificial role on all of our life teams.

Life is about teamwork. And it's vital for me to value the people who invest themselves on my behalf. If you are married, you no doubt realize the role your partner plays. I don't know what I would do if it were not for Barbara's contribution to my life. Because I am always onstage and public with my work, people don't normally see the big picture. Truly the power behind the man, in my case, lies with her. I have already introduced my daughters and the important roles they have played and continue to play for me. I still have my mom as my constant encourager and two brothers who call to remind me from time to time that they love me. I have a mom in-law who has always been there to lend a helping hand. I have a sister in-law and in-Spirit who inspires and amazes me and brothers in-law with whom I have shared some of life's most significant moments. Family is everything.

Then there are life-long friends. George and Karen have been supportive friends for thirty years. They really are getting old! I have already mentioned Michael and his wife Judy who have been constant in friendship for more than a decade. Cecil and I normally touch base once a week just to make sure we are both on track. I have extended family in people like Michael and Karen, Gaylord and Sharon, Bill and Barbara and a host of others literally around the world whom I know are always there. And I haven't really started. There is Hutton, Carol, Larry and Rhesa, Barry and Laurie, Gary and Cynthia. There are those who have become special friends through business like Sheila and Larry, Jan and Bobby, Ken, Tom and Karen, Billy and Betty, Kathy, Pete and Jodie, Joan, Vic and Kim, Witt and Pat, Ken, Glen, Kim, Jeff, and the list goes on.

If this is beginning to read like a personal chapter of appreciation, you are right. It is for me. It is dangerous for me to even begin to name names because I know that I will leave someone out. My purpose is for you and me to be inspired by the reality of the teams we have around us in life. I have to confess that I go too long between times of recognition like this. Take a minute. Sit down and begin to make your list. Get in touch with your life team. Who has been there for you? Who is there for you now? Who do you look to for leadership? Who are your mentors?

I just finished reading a great book about the relationship between Andrew Hill and John Wooden entitled *Be Quick, but Don't Hurry!* Hill played basketball for Wooden at UCLA during their incredible string of national championships. In reality, he rode the bench for four years. This is a book about how and what he eventually discovered through the years he spent with Coach Wooden. It is so inspiring to me to read about the personal relationship between this student and his life-long mentor.

I was touched and inspired by Mitch Albom's book *Tuesdays with Morrie*, a little book that illustrates how a relationship can be built between people who are willing to engage the process. I have already mentioned in the introduction the mentoring I received through men like my father-in-law, Bill Boyar, and my tennis coach, Cal Hopkins. I currently have been blessed with a spiritual mentor in Bill New who has taken a personal interest in me and to whom I look for spiritual challenge and insight.

Two years ago, I was speaking for a company and had the opportunity to meet Ed Schollmaier, former CEO for Alcon. He spoke half the day, and I spoke the other half. I sat in on his session and was immediately impressed with the wisdom and humility of this man. The personal power that illuminated his presentation is hard to describe. I asked to meet with him a few weeks later and asked him to be a mentor to me. He was humbled and surprised, which underscored why he qualified, in my book. I can't tell you how much I gained from the time he was willing to invest in me. Thanks, Ed.

In another sense, it is important to get in touch with the people who serve on your life team in a more practical sense. For instance, I travel frequently and must depend upon others to make things work for me. I depend upon people to serve me every day, and so do you. More often than not, things just seem to come together through the power of team. I must confess, and Barbara would be the first to tell you that I would feel better if I could call everyone together just to make sure that we are all on the same page. And to the degree that I can, I do. But that is more of a personal issue. People need to be trusted to do their job then be recognized for things normally taken for granted. (Just a side note: Don't mess with people you depend on for service. They really will spit in your hamburger!)

PERFORMANCE: IDENTIFYING AND INVESTING

Great relationships don't just happen. They have to be built. They have to be done on purpose. Much like your health, it is not natural to have great relationships in this life. We are far too selfish as human beings for that. The place to begin is to recognize the people who are on your life team and then purpose every day to make some kind of an investment in them. Remember, team includes anyone who you depend upon for your success. Think about it. Who is on your team?

Family

Marriage requires an investment—it's not easy. So taking time daily for your life partner only makes sense. I have spoken to some people who are alienated by the idea of planning time with their spouse. They think that it takes away from spontaneity. If spontaneity is working for you, go with it, but the truth is, most of us don't do spontaneity very well. I think spontaneity needs to be that exceptional moment that creates magic when it happens. However, if you don't have the foundational investment to build on, the magic moments are always going to be too few and far between. Barbara and I have learned that if we do not set up a regular date with each other, it probably won't happen. It's hard to understand how you enter into an arrangement to assure that you will be able to spend more time together, and then you are faced with the reality that the dynamics that develop in the relationship, children as an example, oftentimes serve to keep you from being able to spend time together. It could go without saying, but I better say it because of just how important it is: Never miss those special days in your relationship, like birthdays and anniversaries. It simply has to be done on purpose. You cannot imagine the damage that's done in marriages where love is not continually recognized and remembered.

The rest of your family demands the same purposed attention as your marriage. As I mentioned, having three daughters has taught me the importance of recognizing and respecting the individuality and the uniqueness of people. Another thing I have learned from my time with the girls is the value of shared quality times. When we were preparing to leave South Africa we asked each of our girls to discuss with us their most prized memory about our time in the country. The two oldest girls reflected upon two great holidays we took together. One was to Krueger National Park and the other was into the Draakensburg Mountains. We were given the opportunity to see so many incredible sights during our stay, and that is why Meredith's comments were so meaningful and convicting to me. Her memory was of the time that she and I spent together in a little restaurant called Steak Burger City. Trust me, the quality of the food we ate was questionable to say the least, but it wasn't the food that made the difference to her. Rather it was the quality of the time we spent together, just the two of us.

I have also learned from family that establishing tradition can be a real investment in your relationships. I have always used Valentine's Day as one of those traditions in my relationships with Barbara and the girls. I know you might think this isn't too original, and it really isn't. But I can't tell you how many men I meet who don't understand how important a statement of love is to their relationship on this day. If you think it is cheesy and unnecessary, let me help you focus on their need and not upon your prejudice. By the way, I think fathers and sons can establish the same kinds of traditions. It might be making a tradition out of going to the opening day of baseball season or a regular day for fishing. Whatever you choose will work as long as it becomes something you share on a personal level with the people you love most.

Sooner or later you will also experience a new relationship challenge in your life—aging parents. I lost my father several years ago, but I am blessed to still have my mother. Living and healthy in her seventies, her needs and my attention are probably more important to her now than ever before. If you are like me, it is all too easy for life to go racing by, and somehow she can get lost in the process. On one of my trips, I bought a simple card and sent it to her. Several days later, she called in tears. I was initially concerned until I realized she was calling to tell me that she had just received my card. It doesn't take much, but it is something that has to be done on purpose or it will not happen.

I have two brothers I love, but we rarely communicate. I know it causes Mom undue concern. Not long ago, I received a call from my middle brother, just checking in, and specifically calling to tell me that he loved me. I quickly affirmed the same to him. He then shared with me how he had just spoken to Mom and that she was concerned about how little contact we were maintaining as brothers. After a few moments of reflecting upon Mom's needless concern, we recognized together that we both maintained relationship with others on a regular basis. Somehow it did reflect upon how much value we were placing on this life relationship. It is a commitment and a choice that must be made, otherwise it will be a relationship that will not be enjoyed.

Friends

Friendship and acquaintance are not the same. I am blessed to have people in my life who have chosen to invest in me as a friend. Cecil is a guy who has modeled for me the importance of commitment and contact to the friendship process. On a regular basis, he just calls to check in on me. I have tried to do the same with important friendships in my life. I have found that it is really hard to keep a lot of active friendships going at any one time. It just becomes a physical and emotional impossibility. I do believe, however, that there are friendships in this life that can be maintained by periodic contact just to serve as a reminder of what you mean to one another. I recently attended the funeral of a great friend and a great man. The number and the nature of the people who attended in his memory were a tribute to his impact in their lives. Because of history and family we have shared, there were people present whom I had not seen in years. Yet the relationships, even in memory, continue to be meaningful. I found that so often death creates powerful reunions that life somehow does not produce. The result of this reunion was a recommitment to people we have not seen in a long time. Friendships represent the greatest wealth we will know in this life, and they can also play a big role on our life teams. They will not just happen, however, they have to be done on purpose.

Coworkers

Professional life is probably the most obvious laboratory for team, and yet it is also the arena where it can be the most challenged. Because we have this natural tendency to look out for ourselves and for our own interests, working with others is a daily challenge. But it's essential to your professional success to invest in the people whom you depend upon for your success. In fact, you might need to approach it initially from a bit of a selfish vantage point. What impact will you experience if the people you work with don't do what they do well? It only makes sense that you invest yourself in them, if for no other reason than the positive impact it will ultimately have upon you and what you do.

I talk to people all of the time in organizational America who literally shoot themselves in the foot every day because of the negative impact they are having upon those who work around them. It also happens along departmental or professional lines. Departmental, professional, or organizational prejudice can destroy any organization. I am familiar with one organization that had a major feud going on between their manufacturing and sales departments. Out of spite, they would not get along or communicate. As a result of this self-imposed abuse, there was a multimillion dollar error made in the manufacturing and inventory needs of the organization, creating a major financial impact. You can never be too large an organization to get outside the potentially fatal reach of people pettiness, abuse, and neglect. Teamwork is essential to great corporate performance, yet it is not a natural production. It must be done on purpose out of mutual agreement and shared commitment.

BRINGING TEAM TOGETHER

You have no choice about being on a team. But you do have a choice about how you respond to the reality of team in life. In fact, you are the only one who can. So the challenge of being and doing team is one you need to accept.

As you consider life today, who are the people upon whom you depend for your success? Once you have identified who they are, identify the strategy you are employing to encourage their success. The purpose of this exercise is not to put you on some kind of guilt trip. If you are like me, you will be convicted quickly that there are many people whom you love and depend on who get very little support from you. The purpose of this exercise is to help you get clarity about the priority decisions you need to be making. You have so many demands for your time, and purposed choices can cut down on much of life's confusion and frustration. Team requires your purposed attention if it is going to work well for you. Take the challenge. Be a team builder. The payoff for you will be significant. The value to the people in your world will be immeasurable.

TAKE THE CHALLENGE

This is my challenge: Take the time right now to identify your life team. Get started on the right track by putting your own name at the top of the list. If you need to identify part of your team in groupings, at least get their significance to you clear in your mind. Focus on the people in your life you know you depend upon for your success. They need you, and you definitely need them.

AFFIRMATIONS

I know my team.
I believe in my team.
I need my team.
I am committed to the success of my team.
I will invest time in my team.
I will recognize and praise my team.

SERVANT-
MINDEDNESS

I love to walk into stores where a particular counter or kiosk identifies itself as the go-to place for customers to get help. But many times, no attendant is even there. And if an employee is there, you can bet it's a high school student. In an increasing number of cases, people on duty are disengaged or resent the fact that you have interrupted their day by walking up to their counter. One particular national pharmacy retail chain, who will go unnamed for the protection of the innocent and for me who might be sued for slander, amazes me with their consistency of poor service. You might wonder why I keep going back, and that is a good question that deserves an answer. Unfortunately, the answer is convenience, and I hate it when I say it. For the sake of convenience, I guess I am willing to be underwhelmed. Sad, huh?

One evening, I was sent on an errand to pick up some much needed medication for one of my grandchildren. I knew I was cutting it close, but I thought I would be able to make it before closing. When I arrived I was pleased to see that they were open but disappointed at the number of people in line waiting to be served. I got in line like all good cattle, I mean people, should, and I waited my turn. Barbara hates to be in that situation with me because it is not beyond me to let out a moan resembling a cow as we gradually move forward in line. Sometimes I will even make the sound as though I had just been given the shock of a prod as I inch forward in the line. I realize it is childish, but what can I say; I hate lines. Getting back to the story, there was a woman in front of me who was carrying a purse the size of carry-on luggage. When it was her turn at the counter she was not ready with her checkbook. The young woman behind the counter, somewhere in her teens, rebuked the woman for not being ready and asked her to step aside. I couldn't believe it. As I stepped up for my turn, she turned her attitude to me and demanded, "Next!" I first asked her how she earned the badge she was proudly displaying on her dress. Glancing down to see what I was talking about, she was wearing a name badge that identified her as a "customer service specialist." I asked her how she achieved that designation. She didn't know how to respond to my question, so I asked to see her manager just so I might learn more about the training that was responsible for this impressive experience. She quickly informed me that she was the manager. I knew my efforts were futile—I was doomed to the disappointing experience of being a customer.

Customer service has become a major dynamic in our lives. We are impressed by it, frustrated by it, invested in it, dependent upon it, and more often than not we stay confused by it. No matter where you go or what you do, someone will be serving and someone will be a customer. Our economy depends upon the success of this service sector. More has been written on this subject in the past ten years than ever before. Great companies have been identified and idolized for the kind of service they provide. Their strategies have been dissected and studied. Yet, everywhere I go, the report is the same: Customer service has never been worse.

I realize that there are those exceptional moments that you and I have both experienced as customers where we were pleasantly surprised by the spirit and class with which we were approached. Why does it seem to be the exception? And, if it is the exception, and I am certainly trying to suggest that it is, then doesn't it present a great opportunity for those serving professionals who are trying to provide a "distinctive" presence in the marketplace? The following progression is meant for those of you who are seeking to make that distinction.

PHILOSOPHY: SEIZING AND SERVING

The reality is, there is great opportunity every single day to serve people. We all need it. Some of us need it more than others. And many, if not most of us in this country, are privileged enough to be able to pay for it. It all begins with recognizing this significant reality: We have all been created both to serve and be served.

One of my very first opportunities as a consultant was *We have all been* to work with an organization that sold professional servic- *created both to* es. The owners wanted me to address their customer serv- *serve and be* ice. I was delighted with both the topic and the potential for *served.* the relationship. I spoke one day to half of the company and the next day to the other half. After being introduced, I thanked the owners for the opportunity, and then I related to the organization the assignment I had been given. I then asked one of the owners to help me; I asked him to take out a business card and read aloud what it said, focusing specifically on his title. He very patiently complied. Once he had identified himself as president and CEO, I asked him to take a pen and strike the designation he had on the card and to write in its place the word *servant.* I then went around the room and asked a number of people from a number of different departments and positions to do the same thing. I then announced: Customer service is not a program. It's a lifestyle. It is a relational statement. I then asked them to do a two-minute drill with me at their tables. I asked them to quickly discuss how they felt about their new designation as servant. They did just that. I then went around the room and asked them to give me their one-word reaction to this new identity statement. The overwhelming sense around the room was that they hated it. Reactions included words like "victim," "abused," "used" and "loser." While there was the token sentiment that helping people would no doubt be taking place, the majority vote would not have been positive. Of course, my point was made and it was dramatically seen and felt by this group of employees. I went on to point out that because they had chosen to become professionals in that industry and because they had seized upon serving the needs of people as a means through which they could support themselves and their families, they needed to truly embrace the choice they had made. I will tell you that this epiphany served to significantly change and impact the culture of that company for some time. While continual reinforcement is essential, beginning with this one critical reality is where successful customer service is born.

Amazingly, when you put serving the needs of others into a historical perspective, you find that the most admired and revered people of all time have been thought of as servants. Jesus has been my answer to life's spiritual questions, but he's also my model for service. To me, the attractiveness of his life revolved around his simple commitment to loving and serving the people in his world. Picture Jesus taking a towel and washing the dirty feet of those who considered him their Master and Teacher—that gives overwhelming insight into the power of his serving touch. By seizing the converting power of service, people have literally changed the world. Think about the impact of the call to national service given by President Kennedy with his simple words, "Ask not what your country can do for you but what you can do for your country." Think about the world-changing impact of the Red Cross, Habitat for Humanity, Amnesty International, Optimists, Rotarians, and all of the service organizations of the world. Think about the power in the little woman who chose to walk in the midst of disease and poverty in Calcutta to care for those in need. Kings of the world came to sit at Mother Teresa's feet. There is a power that only comes through a heart that is really committed to serving.

I have been fortunate to experience the power of service firsthand. In many ways it is the legacy left me by my parents: I witnessed it in the commitment of my father, who worked as many as three jobs at one time to provide financially for us. I experienced it in the companionship of my mother at 4:00 A.M. as I tried to throw a rural paper route to make money for tennis lessons. Some of my earliest memories involve my father's combining selling and service. Every year for as far back as I can remember, I helped Dad in selling candy and Christmas trees through Optimists International to benefit young people in need. There were always families in need or schools looking for help, and my dad was right there. My world was defined by servants like my parents, Bonnie and Fred Tappe, as well as Joy and Bill Boyar, Thelma and Dick Heinlen, Cal Hopkins, Herbert Kerbow, Charles Williams, Connie and Byron Zirkle, and on and on I could go. Because of their power, I carry in my heart a commitment to serving the people in my world. My commitment and my life's work is inspired through the lives of people, some of whom may have been poor by world standards, but who were made powerful by their serving hearts.

Customer service is not some program de jour. In fact, it is not restricted to the marketplace. In the previous chapter on team, I suggested that anyone you need to help you succeed should be considered part of your team. Likewise, I believe anyone you depend upon for success needs to be recognized and served as your customer. It really is a powerful paradox. To be successful, you need them to serve you, but unless you are willing to play a role in serving them, you won't succeed. It's like this, as I

> *Likewise, I believe anyone you depend upon for success needs to be recognized and served as your customer.*

travel from place to place, I need people with American Airlines to be effective servants for me, or I won't reach my destination and my speaking engagements. At the same time, they need my cooperation and commitment to them so they can do their jobs properly. In my marriage, I see Barbara as my customer and I am hers. The same goes for my children, my friends, my church, and my community.

Customer service for organizations, however, does have two distinct roles. There is service to those commonly thought of as *external customers*. This traditional category needs little more by way of explanation, although a lot by way of attention.

Secondly, there is service to those now commonly recognized as *internal customers.* The internal customer is anyone who is working alongside you in your world. Certainly that involves those who are your corporate colleagues. Herb Kelleher and Southwest Airlines have been widely recognized for their outstanding customer service. I heard Herb say once that early in his career he had been involved in debate on where to begin with the challenge of customer service. Many suggested that the only answer was to focus on the customers holding the money in their hands. To the contrary, Kelleher said that he has maintained throughout his career that the first and most important customer to be served and cared for is the employee. His conviction is that if you have a well-served employee, you can be confident that you will have a well-served consumer. How can you argue with success? Southwest Airlines, who by the way has little trouble finding employees, is perennially recognized for their legendary and creative service.

In our fast-paced, ever-changing world, I believe this internal customer definition must be expanded to include all of those people and organizations that might serve as members at any one time. *Virtual teaming,* where people come together around a defined and limited goal or objective and then return to their specific life roles once the project is completed, is becoming a common corporate and life strategy. Outsourcing is becoming more and more acceptable in the marketplace as competitive forces call for the most competitive, effective, and efficient professional response. So as your virtual team becomes a reality, the relationships of those people need to be recognized as important customers.

Serving is a powerful force that can change the world and should be seized upon humbly and confidently for the opportunity that it provides. It meets needs on all sides of the equation: for those who serve and for those who are to be served. While there are times that serving will bring its challenges and confusion, it is important for you to trust the power of its presence. If you have chosen to be a service provider, then embrace the spirit of your profession. If you own or manage a company, then inspire those you lead to have the heart of servant. Cheap substitutes will always be exposed in the heat of the fire.

PERSPECTIVE: PATIENCE AND PREPARATION

Through the heart of a servant, people and their problems take on a different look. Instead of being an imposition, they take on a living importance. Instead of being a personal attack, they become your personal ambition. You know you are there—on purpose—to serve the needs of people, so when you see them coming, they are no longer an obstacle to you, but rather they are opportunity you have invited.

I am amazed by the number of people I meet who stay frustrated by the actions and the attitudes of the people who come to them looking for help. Last night I heard the verdict concerning a case that was very publicly tried on the basis of "air rage." I have already said that because I fly a lot I get to see people at their worst. There's no question that people can be angry and abusive. There's no doubt that guidelines of conduct need to be in place and enforced for the good of all who travel the skyways. But at the same time, we are all customers, often tired and frustrated, and airlines must consider that reality. Have you noticed, something often happens to people when you give them a badge and a uniform. It is really hard to explain, but the Don Knotts/Barney Fife picture comes to my mind. I have seen ticket agents and flight attendants who have enflamed situations by their arrogance and impatience. Somehow they forget that passengers are forced to jump through hoops for them with regard to schedules and requirements, but they aren't really held to the same standard. They are a lot like meteorologists. As long as they are close, that is suppose to be good enough. I have been close before and the flight still left me. I have been close before and they still made me check my baggage. I don't know who was at fault in this much-publicized case of air rage, but I do know that if I had been waiting in an airport for ten hours and someone tried to physically restrain my wife from tending to my child I might have the tendency to react myself.

This is not intended to be a treatise on the deficiency of airline service. I, for one, have enjoyed more good service than bad from my airline friends. The issue is expectations. What do airline professionals expect of their passengers? What do medical professionals expect of their patients? I work with a large number of medical professionals, and it is amazing how easy it is for them to become impatient with their patients. People come to them because they are dealing with unexpected and unwanted pain, and yet they are supposed to be polite and sensitive to protocol that all too often has been ineffectively communicated. What do real estate agents expect of their sellers? Of their buyers? Because I have worked so personally with the real estate community, I know how easy it is to get frustrated with people who are stressed about finances and physical transitions.

So what is the answer? Get rid of them. Get rid of all of the passengers, patients, and people who are in need of professional services. If you want to talk about economic recession and depression, let all of the service customers of the world disappear.

Service doesn't restrict itself to the marketplace. I will never forget an experience I had a number of years ago. I had a friend who was truly one of a kind. When God made Mike, he truly broke the mold. There could not be two of this guy in the world. He had an incredible wit and absolutely no inhibition about exposing inconsistency in the world around him. Those of us who were closest to him also knew that we were always subject to this creative and cutting wit. On one occasion, Mike and I set out for the shopping mall to get some last-minute Christmas shopping done. On our way into the mall, we witnessed a mother having trouble with her three-year-old who was flopping in the floor, obviously tired of the whole Christmas-shopping experience. (Where is Santa Claus anyway?) Flopping in her own way, the mother was standing over the child loudly screaming at him and jerking him around. I knew what was about to happen. Mike had a special place in his heart for children. Now get the picture concerning my friend:

Standing about 6'4" and weighing in at somewhere around 375 and on a mission, Mike walked over to the woman and joined with her in yelling at her child. He was yelling even more loudly than she was at the child. He started telling him to grow up and quit acting like a three-year-old. I just knew some policeman was going to escort Mike out of the place! Mike quickly turned his drama to the woman who was absolutely stunned, as a crowd had gathered, and he basically suggested she either love and accept her child as a three-year-old or give him to someone who would. In his own dramatic way, he made the point I want to make in this chapter. We lost Mike all too soon; he died a very young man. Not everyone appreciated his candor, and at times he was hard to deal with, but I always loved his passion for life and his commitment to children. There is even a public park in Mike's hometown named in his memory.

I have great sympathy in the world for people who have trouble in their marriages. Marriage is a challenge—just ask Barbara. I have no patience for those who would stand in judgment over those who have broken marriages. But for God's grace, it could be mine. My point is this: If you don't really want to commit to another person for life, through the good times and the bad, until death do you part, then don't do it. If you do, however, don't throw in the towel when the bad times come. Some of the greatest life tragedies I have witnessed have revolved around marriages that have come apart because one of the partners was not willing to endure the bad times. It is like all of the commitments in the beginning meant nothing. The bad times come. No exceptions.

If you see life from the perspective of a servant, you have more patience in the relationships of life you create. You will also prepare yourself for the challenging realities that they each will bring your way. Customer service professionals will begin to expect and prepare for the challenges that will come their way each day. Parents will give greater thought to having children, and if they are chosen to be the steward of another life then they will pay greater attention to the process required for the development of their children. Marriage partners will reconnect with their vows and will prepare themselves spiritually, emotionally, physically, and professionally to deal with the difficult times that will come.

It is important for you to know that everything I have presented in this chapter I accept as a personal challenge first. I will also be the first to confess my ongoing challenge with the process of being a life servant. I definitely have my moments! I remember my thoughts about Dr. Scott Peck when I read his book *The Road Less Traveled*. I couldn't believe this guy. By implication, I thought he was claiming to be able to walk this "road less traveled." I didn't have much time for Peck after that first reading experience. Years later, however, when I read his very personal work *In Search of Stones*, I was brought to tears as I read the confessional of a man who felt the burden of people like me who had judged him by implication to be some kind of life guru. He wanted the decks to be cleared and for his reading public to know that he was no guru. He wanted everyone to know of his fallibility. I heard him interviewed and heard him express just how important that was to him at this point in his life. His stock went up big-time for me. In fact, the problem wasn't with him. It was with me. I judged him by implication and intention, and I owe him an apology. I'm sorry, Scott.

I realize this life is a process that will never result in my personal perfection. Only a spiritual foundation will answer my need for perfection. But I do believe that by accepting the reality of your created purpose as a servant and by living through those eyes every day, life changes. You become more relationally competent and invested. You become more prepared to deal with the hand life brings your way. Ultimately, you prepare to die. In a crazy kind of way, serving people in life will help you prepare for the service you will need from others in death.

> *Remember, what you see is a product of what you believe, and what you believe is a product of what you have chosen to believe.*

Serving really becomes your vision in life, because you recognize that through serving others you will ultimately be served. It really is a bit selfish—or at least self-serving—at its base, yet it works because everyone benefits from the serving relationship. Instead of resenting the people who look to me for the serving role they need me to play in their lives, I can choose to see them as serving partners who work together to make this world work for everyone. Remember, what you see is a product of what you believe, and what you believe is a product of what you have chosen to believe. Your vision about serving others will improve as you begin to see yourself as a servant in this world.

PERFORMANCE: PREPARE AND DELIVER

Based upon a heartfelt belief in serving the world around you and with eyes that see people as opportunity instead of opposition, you are ready to deliver. In fact, there is a passion that you will begin to feel within yourself that will cause you to desire the challenge of meeting others at their point of need. While there is no bad place to begin, the role you play in serving the world around you will have to be approached from a point of priority or it can actually become a bad place to be.

Every time you say yes to someone or something, you are simultaneously saying no to someone or something else.

I want to share with you a thought that I hope will become an axiom to you as a life servant. Every time you say yes to someone or something, you are simultaneously saying no to someone or something else. We have never lived in a time when there were more people-needs to be met. Your world is filled with them, and it is essential to begin every day by knowing you will not be able to meet them all. Too many people live in bondage to this world through good servant hearts. People will use you and affirm you right into the grave, or at least into a personal crisis. They will not be doing it out of meanness, but rather out of need. You must be the professional and be the one who is purposed about both who and what you can serve in your life.

It is also important for you to accept and approach your life-serving roles as a process. You will never get it all done in a day primarily because we very seldom have "it" well defined. In the previous chapter, I asked you to identify your life team. That done, now what? If you are like me, you probably have a serious list of people who you know you need to be serving more effectively than you are. Remember, guilt is *not* the desired result of this exercise. Accept the fact that you will never be able to do everything you would like to be doing for the people in your world and on your team. The important thing is that you are not paralyzed in the process. Don't allow yourself to be overwhelmed—just get started and see each day as another opportunity to begin again.

In the next chapter, I'll challenge you with a personal planning strategy that will speak more specifically to prioritizing and purposing your life. For now, I believe the most important first step you can take in serving your team is to anticipate their needs. Look at your list. Take them one at a time and identify at least one thing about each one of them that you know they need from you. Think about it from their vantage point. I believe that the development of anticipative skills and the ability to truly empathize with people is the proverbial cutting edge in customer service. It will not only make us more relevant to their world, it will also serve to remove stress and frustration in your own. There will be fewer surprises. You will be more confident in the face of the chaos that serving others will always produce. More significantly, you will be placing yourself in a proactive place of response as opposed to always being reactive.

I believe that the development of anticipative skills and the ability to truly empathize with people is the proverbial cutting edge in customer service.

At the same time, I think it is important for you to get honest about some of the people challenges you face most often that continue to frustrate you. Think about it. If you can clearly identify the challenges you know you will continue to face, why would you not choose to make preparation for meeting them? I work with customer service professionals all the time who continue to allow themselves to be frustrated by the same life situations over and over again. I love to see the transformation that takes place when people get prepared to perform. It is a simple concept yet difficult to apply. If couples could become more prepared to meet the challenges they know they will face with one another, life would be much more peaceful. How many times have you found yourself fighting over the same thing over and over again? Barbara has a personal tendency to talk her thoughts through out loud. There is nothing wrong with it unless and until I try to insert myself into her thought process. I have known and loved her for over thirty years, and yet I still tend not to let her work through her thoughts without interrupting and drawing premature conclusions for her. Requiring her to make a change in her approach to facing life's challenges is not the answer. Barbara is my life customer. I am the one who has to become more disciplined and prepared to play my part in her process. Playing the part I want her to play because I want her to play it my way sounds a lot like abusive customer service approaches I experience every day.

The same observation can be made in all of your life relationships. If you know what to expect, prepare and deliver a purposed response. If you know what to expect from your children, don't allow yourself to become repeatedly frustrated by the same thing. Prepare to meet the challenge. If you know what to expect from the people working around you, don't allow yourself to fall into the same reactive trap day after day. Prepare and deliver a response that is both positive and productive. Remember, if they are on your team, serving them is the best thing you could possibly do for yourself.

GIVING THE PERFORMANCE OF YOUR LIFE

Giving the serving performance of your life should be your goal every day. To the same degree that you accomplish your goal, your life will be an overwhelming blessing both to the world around you and to the world within you. For that goal to be achieved, you have to choose every day. You have to choose not to react to the people around you, but rather to embrace them as life partners. You must anticipate the challenges you know you will experience and prepare to meet them. Choose today to mentally visualize tomorrow. Think about the people who you know will be a part of that experience and reflect upon the kind of things you can expect because of their uniqueness. Choose to see them as distinctive points of diversity as opposed to problems. Develop a strategy in your mind for the performance you believe would represent the best and most productive service contribution for their lives. Practice by reviewing in your mind the way you want it to go. Then, stand and deliver. Don't make excuses. Don't react. Just stand and deliver the personal and professional life performance you know you want and need to provide for your world.

TAKE THE CHALLENGE

Commit each evening for the next thirty days to anticipate the serving challenges you will face the next day. As you anticipate, identify the response you intend to make to the serving challenges that will no doubt come your way. Mind it through. You will sharpen your anticipative skills in the process, and you will become increasingly more confident and positive as a servant.

AFFIRMATIONS

I choose to serve the people in my world.
I will invest in the people who are on my team.
I will anticipate and prepare.
I will celebrate the distinctiveness of the people on my life team.
I will seize the opportunity to help others meet their challenges.
I will stand and deliver.

BALANCING LIFE

Life balance seems like an oxymoron doesn't it? Most groups I work with report that life seems to be moving out of control. It seems to be moving faster and faster like some runaway train. In reality, life is moving no faster. The clock is moving at the same pace as it did last year and the year before. Time may be moving no faster, but we sure are! We are the train out of control. And indicators would suggest that we are about to come off of the track.

A recent survey I read suggested that over 50 percent of Americans surveyed feel as though they are overwhelmed by life. A Gallup survey showed that over 50 percent of the people in their database reported having no enthusiasm about their jobs. Surprised? Depression has reached epidemic proportions. Children are the latest recognized victims. And maybe they have had to fire some dramatic shots to get our attention. Marriage and family has become a life and relationship challenge that seems impossible to meet. Yet, without healthy family environments where do we develop as people? How do we learn how to do life? Technologically speaking, we have never been more connected as people yet *inter*personally and *intra*personally we have never been more disconnected. What is going on? What can we do about it?

Well, you don't have to be an accomplished historian to look back over your historical shoulder and recognize a staggering trend. For the first nineteen hundred years of human history, there were only three major "ages" of civilization typically recognized. We began with the Stone Age. Physical strength was the control determinant. Some would suggest we haven't moved far from our roots. Power and control continue to be big issues among us. As Alvin Toffler suggested in his book *PowerShift*, the only thing that has really changed is the way we achieve it. Physical strength was our original measure, and it still has its remnant priority among us. We then progressed into the Agricultural Age where we began to produce for ourselves. We also became people who recognized and became recognized by what we produced and owned. Wealth became the source of real power. The "haves" and the "have-nots" became an unfortunate and distinctive life reality. Powerful landowners became the owners of people. And then came the revolutionary Industrial Age in which, unfortunately, many of us have our lives rooted. Darwinian thought moved from scientific observation and obsession into organizational charts and oppression. People became replaceable. People began to leave their farms in order to make a living. Families were separated physically for the first time out of necessity. Urbanization became the new reality. Cities grew. Capitalists built and people came. Some found opportunity while others found abuse. And so the world lumbered along for nineteen centuries.

While this might be a very subjective and simplistic look at those nineteen hundred years, please grasp the concept that change came slowly. Time seemed to move with some degree of dependability and recognition. Although life was difficult, for the most part, the desire for people was for it to move a little faster.

Then came the computer. Dates are debatable, but somewhere around mid-twentieth century, the Information Age began. Punch cards and Hallowith technology became the genesis for a revolution that rolled through the twentieth century and roared into the twenty-first. The engine and energy for the runaway train that we each have become is the computer. Technology has become our taskmaster. It needs us to operate it, yet in many ways it has a life of its own. With great frustration, it waits for people to jump onboard. With each new development, the pace gets faster. In fact, we are now birthing "ages" every few years. What took nineteen hundred years for us to do before, we are now accomplishing within ten. We have rapidly moved from the Information to the Digital Age. Some would suggest that we have already progressed into the Biotechnical Age. Who knows what is before us, but whatever it is, it is coming fast!

The historicity of these observations may be arguable, but the reality and the effect is not. In *MegaTrends*, a book written in the early 1980s by John Naisbitt, an emerging social trend was recognized. Naisbitt and his colleagues suggested that technology would indeed be the taskmaster it has become and that it would require ever-increasing investment and attention. At the same time they warned that corresponding and complementary attention and investment would need to be paid to and made toward "people" as an asset in order for us to handle the life challenges that "high-tech" would create. In 2000, they produced another work entitled *High Tech, High Touch.* I'll give you a very brief synopsis: "We told you so!" The advice was not heeded. Corporate America was being enamored by the new capacity technology provided. Potential for increased productivity and corresponding profitability blinded executive eyes. Then there was the all too obvious failure of the re-engineering and empowerment movements. There is similar surprise today about the insecurity being felt in the workplace and the corresponding instability that it has produced. The majority of the American workforce are "disengaged" from their jobs. People want desperately to believe that they are making a difference. Unfortunately, the never-ending grind we are experiencing seems to be suggesting something else.

It is time for a change. It is time for the players to take responsibility for themselves and for their personal security in this life. We have to quit looking for someone to blame. It is also time for those who are playing organizational leadership roles in our world to respond to the people who are looking to them for signals. By embracing the purposed progression I recommend in this chapter, you will see positive results both personally and organizationally. I guarantee it!

PHILOSOPHY: VALUE AND PROTECT

People are the most valuable "supernatural" resource we have in this world. There is only One who is still making people, and he places a high value on his work. We need each other to get into this world, even with God's creative power. People are incredible. We have power, potential, and possibility that no computer will ever replicate. Families, communities, governments, institutions, organizations, and corporations are all built upon us. We are "people-centric" in this life, no matter what science or technology does to improve things for us. So what is the point? How much do you value *you*? How much do you value the people in your world? Evidence would suggest that we do not actively recognize people as life's most precious resource either on a personal or on an organizational level.

It really begins with you and with what you believe *You will be treated* about you. I realize that self-image is no new discussion. *no better by others* However, in this progression I would like to go behind *than you treat* how you see yourself to what you believe about yourself. *yourself.* Do you believe that you are an asset of great value? Do you believe you are worth personal attention and investment? Do you believe that you are distinctive? In reality, the most abusive person to you is probably you. It is time for you to make the choice to change that relationship. You will be treated no better by others than you treat yourself. The way you allow others to treat you will be a significant reflection of your life philosophy.

I have been amazed in working with abuse victims through the years to see how often they ultimately conclude that they are somehow responsible for the abuse they are experiencing. I had the opportunity to work with a young mother who had just survived being beaten nearly to death with a barstool by her husband. She barely escaped with her life. Yet, after she and her children had enjoyed a brief respite from the terror, she began to reason that his actions were her fault. She must have provoked him. Her provocation must have produced this punitive reaction on the part of her husband. Ridiculous! He did what he did because he chose to, and she was reasoning the way she was reasoning because she was not confident to reason otherwise. We need to think about life through minds that are totally convinced of our own personal value as well as of the value of those around us. Respect is the result of that kind of reasoning. Self-respect will then breed a respect for others that will produce a new life response.

Organizations must change the way they think about the people who work for them. They spend a great deal of time investing in organizational development but very little time in the development of the people who are the organization. I am almost sure that this observation will draw a quick reaction from those who would point to the plethora of training opportunities that so many companies provide. Corporate America must recognize that the people of your organizations look at your training efforts as something that is being done for the organization and not for themselves. It is all about the organization and not about the people. They feel victimized by your training and development efforts because they do not believe that it is about them. They believe it is being done to them. The best thing you can do for your organization is to invest in the people of your organization as *people*. If they develop and become healthier as people, the serendipity will be that your organization will benefit and grow. It has to be about them, however, before it will ever make any real difference.

The best thing you can do for your organization is to invest in the people of your organization as people.

I have had the opportunity to work with thousands of employees, and I have become accustomed to their typical reaction to what is initially believed to be "just another training program." In fact, I typically begin my programs by asking them to tell me just how high their attendance and involvement in this training opportunity ranks on their "gag me" meter. Although that kind of beginning might seem a little tough for those of us who make our living training others, I believe it is the most honest place to begin. After listening to them over a lot of years, I have become sympathetic to their plight. They are required, or "encouraged," to participate in something that is going to put them further behind in meeting the productivity requirements of the very organizations that are requiring their attendance. They would rather be out there getting the job done than sitting in some room getting further behind. Somehow there is too often a disconnect between corporate training and personal value.

Once companies begin to invest in the health and in the well-being of their most valuable asset, people will begin to perform from a performance base of personal pride and from a positive sense of self-worth.

PERSPECTIVE: EXPECTATION AND EXPERT

Once you become convinced of your personal value, you begin to see life through new eyes. Think about how that principle works in the rest of your life. I drive an expensive automobile that I really enjoy. There is no question that it is a personal indulgence, although I do not care to discuss it. However, I keep a pretty close eye on the dashboard indicators to make sure that I get it in for the service that I am told it requires. Because of how much I love this car and because of how much it is worth, it would be totally irresponsible of me to allow it to fall into disrepair. I am afraid I treat my car a lot better than I do myself. How about you?

We recently had a fire in our house. It started in our bedroom, and if we had not discovered it when we did, the damage could have been much worse. Alarms worked the way they were intended. We were warned and disaster was diverted. When I bolted into the bedroom and through shocked eyes saw the fire that had erupted next to our bed, my first impulse was not to put out the fire. Instead, my attention immediately went to the two guitars that were in their cases against the wall right next to the fire. At some risk, I rushed in and moved those prized possessions before any damage could come their way. Fortunately, we were able to put the fire out as well. But I have to tell you that my number-one concern was to protect the possessions I valued most in that room. I love those guitars. One of them is an old Gibson that is over fifty years old and twenty-five of those years have been with me. The other one is a beautiful Martin guitar that is also a treasured gift from Barbara. The point is that when you really value something you do what you have to do to protect it.

Each day you have choices to make about how you treat yourself. How much sleep you get, how much food you eat, how much nourishment you give your heart and mind will all happen as a result of how you see you. Are you the most valuable possession in your life? It is at this point that people begin to get a little uncomfortable. It happens to spiritually

Valuing yourself is a prerequisite to true humility.

minded people in specific, because humility is such a big part of their program. Many would suggest that if you see yourself as being incredibly valuable, somehow that is translated into arrogance. If humility is something you hope to achieve in your life, here is something you must realize. Valuing yourself is a prerequisite to true humility. Any sense of humility that is predicated upon a perspective of personal deficiency will breed abuse. Personal and interpersonal abuse is based in an inadequacy of respect for humanity. Thinking differently about yourself will produce a different kind of relationship for you with yourself and with others.

The same thing is true for organizations of people. You will pay attention to what you respect. You will invest in those things you value. You will protect the things you treasure. Remember that over 50 percent of working America is totally unenthusiastic about work. Millions of dollars are being spent by organizations to "do" enthusiasm to their people. But motivational seminars and "fire walks" are not getting the job done. Why not? If you analyze the word *enthusiasm* you will discover the answer to the question. The word means literally "spirit within" you. You cannot do enthusiasm *to* people. You can't motivate people, at least not for long. It has to begin within them. You have to be sufficiently motivated within before you will ever experience any sustained motivation without.

Too many people in positions of management see their relationship with those they manage in much the same way as too many people see themselves. They believe that when they value their people too much, their people will begin to think of themselves as being worth more than they are. So their erroneous conclusion is not to value their people sufficiently in order to somehow protect the company from the perceived cost of employee arrogance. I am afraid that what I have just described is probably more the rule than the exception in organizational America.

Most managers would do just about anything rather than address compensation issues. Many managers will wait until the employee has become disgusted, disgruntled, and disinterested, and then they will rush in and fix things by giving them a raise. Think about the message that is sending! Compensation is not a people-valuing tool. It is a performance-valuing statement. It is a corporate production strategy. Companies will pay dollars to produce a particular kind of result. The pay people receive is the reflection of a strategy formulated by those who are ultimately responsible for the corporate production of a profitable result. How much they appreciate someone for who they are as a person will not be the determinant. How much they value the performance of the person will be. Too many people are being destroyed today because they are allowing corporate strategy decisions to become the benchmark by which they value themselves. So when they are retired or "reorganized," they have no choice but to take it personally. Managers need to get clear about this fact with those they manage. Only then will they be able to get on with what they really should be about. Here is reality: People will not become professionally arrogant when they are valued and

People will not become professionally arrogant when they are valued and appreciated.

appreciated. Rather, they will become professionally reflective of the way in which they are both seen and treated.

PERFORMANCE: **PROTECTIVE AND PRODUCTIVE**

Because of the value you represent, you have to be involved in a preventive maintenance program for your life. You cannot afford to wait until you break down to invest in yourself. Nor can you wait on or blame an organization for what they are doing or not doing for you. You have to begin now; you are probably overdue. Life's choices and expectations do not allow you the luxury of down time. Your readiness to perform daily has never been more required, though it's never been more difficult to be ready. Now is the time for you to produce a personal life plan—and to put that plan into effect.

PURPOSED PERFORMANCE LIFE PLANNING

Purposed Performance Life Planning is a simple strategy for living that will work for you. It is built upon the power of a life concept called *centergy.* Centergy means centering your life strategically in your convictions and your commitment. I don't propose a life-planning process that is either inspired or original. I do, however, intend to place before you a plan that is both simple and sure. This is not meant to be a traditional goal-setting exercise; it's not about winning and losing. A Purposed Performance Life Plan is a purposed strategy to prepare yourself for successfully meeting the challenges you have before you. I want to give you a personal tool that will help you achieve the life results you purpose to achieve.

> *Centergy means centering your life strategically in your convictions and your commitment.*

The Purposed Dimension is your foundation as a human being. The place to begin is with an understanding of how you work as a person. On one level you are a single, whole being. On another level you are a multidimensional being, as internally dynamic as you are externally. This is the dimension where your life motivation is developed. It's where you will choose and develop your relationship with *yourself,* where you will make your choices about your identity, your security, and your purpose.

The Physical Dimension is the next piece in this multidimensional challenge. This is the dimension where purposed health is determined and energy is created. It is here that your convictions are given the energy essential to their expression.

The People Dimension is built upon the concept and momentum of these foundational dimensions. This is your relational dimension, where you'll find the support and encouragement you need to give full expression to your convictions. This is about family, friends, colleagues, and community.

The Professional Dimension is last, but certainly not least. This dimension is the public expression of your life. It is in this dimension you are able to showcase what you really believe and who you really are.

These four life dimensions are interdependent in nature. They are equally present and essential, and they directly impact one another. Think about it: If you are depressed and you don't believe that you make any real difference in life, how does it impact your life? Physically speaking, do you sleep too much or too little as a result? Do you eat too much or too little? Do you exercise too much or too little? How do things go in the relationships of your life? What is typically going on for you professionally when your motivation is low? When you are struggling physically how is the rest of your life impacted? Your motivation, your relationships, and your ultimate expression professionally will always be challenged when your physical foundation is shaken. The same rule applies when you are troubled relationally. How do you handle life when family is not going well? Every other part of your life will be impacted. When things are difficult professionally, how often do you begin to question everything about who you are? How is your physical health impacted by increased stress? Unfortunately, you will probably be taking out your stress on the people you love most.

So, now what do you do? Now that we have established that you are impacted by every part of who you are, what do you do? The answer is, you pay attention. You begin to invest in yourself as the valuable asset that you are. You recognize the fact that you are a spiritual being and that you actively invest yourself in discovering the answer to life's most significant questions. You begin to take your physical self seriously. You take time for yourself and for your personal health. You recognize the people around you as the valuable gifts that they are. You invest yourself in their health and development. You see your professional life as daily opportunity for personal expression. You continually look for opportunity to learn and grow in the process. You do for yourself what organizational America has learned to do for itself. You choose your personal mission. You set your course.

I have included at the end of this chapter a Purposed Performance Life Plan worksheet as well as a completed personal sample, not to influence you toward any specific personal plan that I might have, but rather to give you as much practical direction as I can. It is important that you make this planning process a personal project. You cannot get it wrong. I will tell you that most people will tend to think of this process as a goal-setting exercise and, as a result, will not get it done. Why not? Because they have tried it before and they have failed. When is the last time you have made a serious New Year's resolution? Maybe you are one of those people who have given up.

Anchor Points get you in touch with an important balancing energy in your life-planning process. An anchor point is action you take that will keep you on a purposed course. Purposed Performance Life Planning asks you to set some important anchor points for each dimension of your life, not so you can keep score, but so you won't be blown too far off course by life.

If you have done any boating, you understand the significance of anchoring. I love the story that I heard about Max Lucado, a great, best-selling Christian author. Years ago, while Max was living in Miami, he and his roommates decided to live on a houseboat. The only problem was that none of them knew anything about living on a boat. When word came that a hurricane was headed their way, they did what most inexperienced people would do. They tied their boat to every solid thing they could find on the dock. An old, experienced boat-man put his arm around Max and explained to him that if that "'cane" blew through, it would destroy everything on that dock. He further explained that his only real hope was to anchor deeply.

I am asking you to throw out some anchors for your life. Don't throw out too many or you might sink. And don't try to sail through too quickly either. This is not a competition. Remember, it is not about being a success or a failure. It is about being awake and alive to the fact that you need to stay on course in this life. It is probably time for you to begin again. Choose to exercise the greatest human power and freedom you possess. Choose to begin again.

Putting It All Together

There is no question as to your value. There is no question as to your potential. The only real question is what are you going to do with what you have been given?

There is no question that as a company your greatest value is found in your people. There is no question as to the untapped potential that they represent. The only real question is what are you going to do with what you have been given?

I challenge you on both a personal and an organizational level: You make the application you need to make. Don't let someone else choose for you how your life needs to be done. You are too significant! There is too much at stake.

Take the Challenge

Create a Purposed Performance Life Plan for yourself. Establish no more than three anchor points for each dimension of your life. Use my sample plan as your guide. If you would like to have themes for each dimension as I have done, then do it. Suggest that everyone on your professional team do the same. Then compare notes. Where possible, develop accountability partners for support. If that cannot be done, or at least is not relationally practical within your team, make sure you have someone who is supporting you in this effort. Invite your manager to become your partner. I am not kidding. Create positive tension for yourself. If you have not already taken the challenge (chapter 5), develop a purpose, a mission, and a vision statement for yourself. Don't put it off. Keep it simple. To help you, answer these questions:

1. Purpose: What am I doing with my life?
2. Mission: Why am I doing it?
3. Vision: Where is it taking me?

AFFIRMATIONS

I am valuable.
I have great potential.
I have a mission.
I have a purpose.
I have a plan.
I will be accountable.

Purposed Performance℠ Life Plan

Purposed Performance Statement:

This year I choose to . . . (purpose)

Because I . . . (mission)

So that I . . . (vision)

Purposed Dimension: I will stay motivated by

1._____

2._____

3._____

Physical Dimension: I will stay healthy by

1._____

2._____

3._____

People Dimension: I will stay relationally strong by

1._____

2._____

3._____

Professional Dimension: I will showcase excellence by

1._____

2._____

3._____

Purposed Performance℠ Life Plan

Allen Tappe

Purposed Performance Statement:

This year I choose to actively celebrate the presence of God in my life, *because* it is in his presence that I will grow in his love *so that I* will be more centered and better prepared to serve the people in my world.

Purposed Dimension: I will stay motivated by

1. Beginning each day with praise and prayer.
2. Listening to God for the opportunities he intends for my life each day.
3. Spending time in God's Word each day and producing at least one new SpiriTalk CD.

Physical Dimension: I will stay healthy by

1. Doing three days of cardio and two days of light-weight and high-repetition workouts each week.
2. Playing tennis weekly and staying competitive.
3. Maintaining a daily vitamin regimen.

People Dimension: I will stay relationally strong by

1. Expressing love to Barbara every day.
2. Encouraging my daughters and grandchildren in their life challenges.
3. Contacting my friends and family each week.

Professional Dimension: I will showcase excellence by

1. Booking 100 days and two successful events for the coming year.
2. Writing and publishing two additional books in the Application Series.
3. Creating an annual business model and strategy for the Institute.

SUCCESS
THROUGH
FAILURE

I have been in some kind of competition since I was five. Every day I can remember of my young adult life I wore pads or bounced a ball, competing in some kind of athletic competition. In fact, the same has been true of my older adult life. Achieving at high levels of performance has been my life experience and rule. It is a rule I live by, greatly overstated, and the rule I expect others to live by as well. On some levels, it has served me well. On other levels, it has been incredibly destructive.

From the very beginning of this book, I have been alluding to and somewhat suggesting a thought to you. It's time for us to deal with it: You are not going to get away from doing things wrong in this life. So get over it! It may be a noble aspiration and at times even a great motivating force to pursue a course without failure or fault, but both in the long and short run, it is a bondage that does far more harm than good.

To operate from the vantage point of having to achieve perfection creates personal pressure for both yourself and the people who must live with you. Just ask the people who live closest to you. If there's one thing in my life that has been the most damaging to both myself and those I love, it would be my impossible standards for performance.

In the April 1996 issue of *Fast Company,* there was a fascinating cover story featuring Mort Meyerson, the then-retired, past president of EDS in Dallas. The article focused upon Ross Perot's attempt to recruit Meyerson out of retirement to lead the troops of his new organization. Meyerson initially declined, telling Perot that he thought he had been out of touch for too long to make any kind of meaningful comeback. After some discussion, however, Meyerson agreed to come back and take a look at things to see if there was a plausible role he felt he could play. This article, entitled "Everything I Thought I Knew about Leadership Was Wrong" overviewed his observations and the discovery that governed his eventual return. In this insightful confessional of sorts, Meyerson communicated the heart of a man who was capable of embracing success through the shadows of his failure. In looking back at the success of EDS, he saw things he could no longer represent as positive leadership among people. He saw some things that he believed he did wrong in leading both customers and employees, even though they had obviously developed into great economic success. He saw things that he would change if he came back to play any kind of role in leading people. Accepting those conditions for making a return, Perot welcomed him back. I am not sure where Meyerson is today in his leadership journey, but I appreciate his spirit and hope he stays alive and alert in his process.

Failure is a strong word. It is an alienating word, one that can be argued by definition. I am using it in this chapter to recognize the powerful disappointment we feel when we allow ourselves to believe that we have done things wrong, when we allow ourselves to believe that what we have done has been done in vain. In reality, failure in life comes only when we cease to learn from our ongoing encounters with it. Choose to adopt the following progression about life for yourself and begin to feel the liberation that a purposed-life failure could produce.

PHILOSOPHY: DISCERN AND DEVELOP

Life is an ongoing development process. Every day produces new experiences that carry new opportunities for learning and development. Daily living must not be considered a win–lose proposition. It must be valued as a win–win possibility. You can't lose if the object of your life is to learn and grow, and you choose to continue to do so. Recognizing your failure—getting it wrong, not getting it right, missing the mark, losing the battle, sin, whatever—is the energy essential to your continued maturity as a human being. With that in mind, think about how much energy you have for growth within yourself.

> *Daily living must not be considered a win–lose proposition.*

My belief system is grounded in a conviction that life is not about failure but about transformation. It is about being taught in such a way through every experience of my life to see the success I already am. I believe that we are all part of a great team presentation in life. That presentation begins and ends with God. The real issue is one of personal security. What is the basis for your security in life? Is it performance based? Are you all right if you do right? What about when you get things wrong? We can't embrace our life failures as opportunity if our failures represent only failure to us. Security is an environmental foundation that we must have on both a personal and a community level if we are to live powerful and purposed lives.

For any security to be truly experienced, you must accept the fact that you are going to fail. There is no question about it. You are not going to be perfect in your performance, so move on. The quest for perfection can be positive if you accept from the beginning your personal inability to achieve it. Every performance in life will give you another chance to see your imperfection, and it will provide you another opportunity for learning and growth. You'll even find opportunity for celebration if you are able to be at peace with your limitations in the process.

Unfortunately, too many people have been raised in families where failure was not tolerated. Report cards with less than A's were unacceptable and punished. If you weren't in first place then you had no place at all. I've worked with professionals trained to believe that they must represent perfection as though it is actually achievable. Their striving creates an immediate bondage both for themselves and for the people in their world. They are expecting something of themselves that is impossible. As a result, their frustrations will be internalized and externalized. As people, we must be about personal process, not about personal perfection. Remember that wrong expectations will always produce wrong relational results.

As people, we must be about personal process, not about personal perfection.

The same thing is true for the organizations in which we live and work. A work environment must be one in which "process" is celebrated. To the same degree that you disallow failure, you also have inhibited performance. Anytime fear is the motivator, positive results will be short-lived. However, where vision is present there will be the power for continual pursuit. Many organizations are actively engaging this challenge. They realize that the productive performance they are hoping to achieve will never be realized through the limiting presence of constant criticism. They are trying to create new cultures that will support the kind of exceptional performance they need from people. In order for that to take place, leadership must be in agreement that the culture will be built on a foundation that celebrates process. People must not be criticized for their lack of perfection as long as they are willing to stay in process. If the risk in failure is too great, people will always gravitate toward a performance in which they will be assured success. The primary reason for resistance to change is the insecurity that it produces. Where failure is punished, people are less likely to accept risk. Words like *innovation* and *initiative* will not be present.

Security among people is the exception; it's not natural. Your security must be grounded in something you can believe in and place your faith in every single day and in every single life situation. To the same extent that security is diminished, performance also will be constrained. So on a personal level, you must choose a faith path that will support you through the security it provides. On a family level, you must be conscious of the foundational impact you have upon one another. You must strive to provide a place where process will be celebrated from the very beginning. Where perfection is required, abuse will always be present. Companies must create environments where people are encouraged and celebrated for their pursuit of excellence. They must build mutual leadership systems that support the process of performance and development.

Purposed vision begins with a heart that is secure.

You must be able to see through eyes that have been trained to see opportunity in every mistake you make. Purposed vision begins with a heart that is secure. Remember, the security you feel will always be based upon the personal choices you make. Living a purposed life must begin with choices that provide security for your process.

PERSPECTIVE: LEARNING AND GROWING

I have a friend who has a great perspective about life. He believes that life is always good. When you see him and ask how he is doing he will either say, "Blessed," if things are going well, or he will say, "Learning and growing!" if things are particularly challenging. Either way, he is going to be smiling, and you somehow know that he is excited about living. Today, I was reminded of a great line of poetry that says, "Life is always right." How do you see life? What do you say when you are asked about how your life is going? When you begin from a place of security, life takes on a new appearance. It does not mean that we go around with a perpetual smile on our face. But even through tears we can have a smile in our heart.

Years ago, I knew a man who chose "terrific" as his personal response to life.

At one point, he and his family went through some particularly difficult situations. People around him had a hard time accepting this seemingly manufactured reply to their inquiries as to his well-being. But he believed he had a choice to make about how he framed the things that were happening to him. He could see them as unfair, unjust, and unnecessary and be depressed. Or he could choose to see them as a necessary part of his life process and be impressed with the possibility every challenge represented. He was secure in making the choice to see life as a gift.

Humility

What do you learn through the failures you experience? One insight you glean through recognized deficiency is personal humility, the beginning point for a powerful life. It sounds contrary, doesn't it? However, you will never have a secure start without humility. You will never be able to learn anything from anyone or anything without a basis point of personal humility. You will never enter into the powerful reality of team without a sense of interdependency and need, and that sensory development must begin from a place of humility.

Victims of the world are people who have never been able to actively embrace personal humility. They will get pitiful down real well, but they will always have someone else or something else to blame. It can never be their fault, because they are not secure enough in themselves to face that reality.

Scott Peck has written a book entitled *Golf and the Spirit*. I have found over the years that I have much in common with Peck. We both have played competitive tennis. We both have worked in the field of human development and performance. And it would appear that we both enjoy a love–hate relationship with the game of golf. Peck says that he plays golf because it causes him to suffer total humiliation. Can I ever relate to that! I have never played a game that I could not achieve at least some measure of excellence. Please do not confuse that comment with arrogance. The truth is that I have been blessed with a great deal of physical and mental ability, and many of life's games have been fairly easy for me. Golf, however, is the clear exception. I have experienced complete humiliation and descended into the depths of despair within its eighteen holes. Of course, I almost always play the last few holes well. That is the hook. But in the process, I have done everything wrong possible up to that point. I have missed the ball altogether in more than one fairly public context. I am finally convinced that I am not a gifted golfer. Since I have come to grips with that reality, however, I have begun to play better. I have actually begun to hit the ball on purpose. I now have an idea where it's going a lot of the time. I don't have to gauge the impact of my slice with each swing. It seems like when I released myself from the bondage of expected perfection in the game, I finally began the process of learning how to play it. Life is a lot like that.

Discernment

Beyond humility, however, you learn something about discernment. No matter what you are considering by way of a failing performance, you no doubt began pursuing a course that you thought might get you where you wanted to go. Now you are in a position to see things differently. There's a perfect illustration of this for those of us who have been blessed with children. Now admit it. When you had your first child, didn't you begin

You become more capable through the acknowledgement and appreciation of your incompetence.

the parenting process a bit arrogantly? You knew how you were going to raise this child, and you weren't going to make the same mistakes you saw your parents make. Now how do you see things? If your child has entered the teen years, I can tell you, you can relate to the humility lesson in a very personal way. If anything can humble a parent, it's a teenager. Because you have been humbled, and because you, like me, have accepted the mistakes you have made in parenting, you're now better able to discern the process before you. It is that simple: You become more capable through the acknowledgement and appreciation of your incompetence.

Thanksgiving

When humility becomes your new filter, and discernment becomes your new capability, thanksgiving will become your new response. Once you embrace your imperfection and begin to discern life through that new lens, you have a deeper appreciation for the success you experience. I love it when a plan comes together. And yes, I do believe that work and planning are necessary in the process. I am just more aware than ever before that if any level of success has been achieved, then I have many to thank and much for which to be grateful. All success in life happens through the orchestrated efforts of many and, while you may have been holding the baton as the conductor, the harmony that you experience far exceeds your production abilities.

I just received a call that explains more clearly what I intend. A woman I have never met called to express her heartfelt appreciation for a CD she had received that I had recorded. She wanted to know where she could get more of this recording and how she could support and encourage the project. The CD, entitled *SpiriTalk*, is a Christian meditation project that began two years ago in the adult Sunday school class I teach in North Richland Hills, Texas. I was impressed with the need for Christians to embrace the power of God's Holy Spirit in their thoughts and in their lives. So, with the help of a gifted musician friend, *SpiriTalk* was birthed. Not sold in stores, and with absolutely no marketing, the CD has gone all over the world and even up to the International Space Station. I contributed to the project not only my ability, but also my lack of ability. Things I thought would work, didn't. I have had so many people try to congratulate me on this effort and I appreciate so much their intent, but I can tell you quickly that I am so thankful to have been a small part of a success that I know is so far beyond my ability to produce. In fact, if it had been limited to my way, it would never have been completed, much less have taken flight. There is a joy that comes through recognizing the bigger picture of which you are simply a part.

Within the last year, on two different and very embarrassing occasions, I missed speaking engagements entirely. I cannot tell you just how frustrating that is to me. It is absolutely *unacceptable*. Yet because of great professional relationships, it became acceptable. Don't get the wrong picture. It was not the plan but it happened. Because, however, of the history we had written together, both company executives literally helped me get over it. They actually consoled me—and they were the customers, the ones mistreated. But they wanted me to see it as a place from which to grow. They wanted to know what we could learn to protect against a similar experience in the future. The relationship actually grew stronger in my estimation as a result of accepted failure and mutual determination to learn and grow from it.

Failure is an illusion. What you see is not what you get, unless you choose to see it that way. In reality, failure is new opportunity for learning and growth. It always provides the elements necessary to help you see yourself and your world through new and more mature eyes. With that view in mind, the rest of the story always represents the experience of a new beginning.

PERFORMANCE: LISTENING AND RESPONDING

Once you embrace failure as a potential friend and not a necessary foe, you are set free. Instead of defeating you, the mistake becomes an enriching learning experience. Even consequences produce new wells from which to draw. Some may read this chapter as an invitation to join the ranks of the mediocre. On the contrary, being set free from the self-imposed *welcome criticism.* bondage of performance perfection allows you to move to that next level of personal achievement, because now you are ready to listen.

The most positive thing you can do for yourself and the world around you is to invite and even welcome criticism.

The most positive thing you can do for yourself and the world around you is to invite and even welcome criticism. How much can you learn if you are not willing to listen to the input that could help you in the process? It goes without saying that not all criticism will be valuable. In fact, some of what you will hear deserves little consideration. That, however, will be the exception. My personal rule is that I pay little attention to extremes on either side of the equation. As a professional speaker, I often receive critiques from the people with whom I have worked. I really do welcome them. When I am allowed to review the written reviews, I ignore the extremes—the people who are overly enamored by me, as well as those who do not like me. I have long since come to grips with the fact that there are some people in this world with whom I was not meant to be. I don't believe those offering the criticism are to be faulted for their opinions; nor do I believe that I need to react to them. I think they should be respected. I am even able to benefit from that extreme criticism through the continuing lesson of humility that it provides. Equally extreme will be those people who think I am the best speaker they have ever heard in their lives. While that opinion may feel a little better, it doesn't offer much for me to work with in the area of learning and growth. In fact, if I were to choose to ignore the negative extreme and embrace the positive, I would quickly become a legend in my own mind. The humility factor is really at risk if I embrace only the extreme positive side. The point is that extremes seldom provide much by way of insight. They can hurt by evoking reaction or they can be processed through the filter of humility and keep you pointed in the right direction.

The people who take the time to offer honest and, to a measured degree, objective criticism are valuable resources. They will be found in the middle and not on either extreme. We make it so hard for people to offer their criticism that most people will avoid the conflict they know they will have to face. At the conclusion of one speaking event, my audience was invited to provide comments about the program. Those in attendance were customers of the organization that was sponsoring me. I stood at the back and met a number of the people on the way out. One woman came up to me and shoved her comment sheet into my hand then walked immediately out the door. I quickly reviewed her comments and then went to inquire about who she was. I was told that she was a new customer, and they were delighted to see her in attendance. When I asked how I might reach her, they were immediately apprehensive about how I might respond to her criticism. I assured them that I wanted to thank the woman for taking the time to provide me a very valuable insight that would help me in my work. I called her that afternoon and was amazed at how concerned she was about my calling. In fact, her first words were, "You were offended by my comments weren't you?" I quickly explained that, far from being offended, I appreciated her taking the time to provide me the insight and opportunity to make a presentational change that clearly needed to be made. I told her that I thought she was on target with her criticisms. She was amazed. She shared that she had never been thanked by anyone for criticism even if it had been invited. I know I have missed many opportunities to thank people who were trying to help me. A person who will invest their time in you should always be appreciated. Think of someone you might need to thank.

Years ago a gentleman came to me with a criticism that was really hard for me to take. I was running for a political office in our community and he wanted to offer me his support. He wanted to help me financially as well as personally. He told me that he noticed that I bit my fingernails. He said that people in the public eye are constantly scrutinized and that chewing my fingernails was a habit that did not represent me well. I did not know what to say. I was embarrassed. At the same time, I was impressed with the level of this person's commitment to me. I am not telling you that moments of criticism are comfortable, but I am telling you that they are powerful if you will embrace them. To this day, I do not bite my nails. I think about him every time I make the choice not to continue that bad habit.

Offering criticism requires great care and finesse. I think it is always wise to proceed with caution when criticizing others. It is how we invite and receive criticism, however, that I want to focus on at this point. The greatest challenge for any manager of people is communication. In specific, how do you provide them effective communication concerning their performance? Providing employees with an honest and adequate review creates a tension that most managers would rather avoid. In fact, most companies I am familiar with really fall short in this area. There is a real dilemma in many organizations. Employees express their desire for better communication and for a more honest and relevant review process from management, but managers avoid communication and the review process in specific because of the conflict that comes with it. Employees must learn that if you want people to help you learn and grow through the insight they provide, you have to make it easy for them to offer it. You cannot crucify them when they offer their criticism to you and then complain when they would rather avoid the process. Without question, companies would become more productive tomorrow, if managers were more capable in communicating through employee reviews and if employees were more open to receiving them.

Approach every day and every person as though you are the student and they are the teacher. Listen to every signal and learn from every insight life and people in your life are willing to give. Because you begin every day secure in the humble fact that you do not know it all nor will you be getting it all right, you can be completely open to the opportunity that each day presents. It is amazing how quickly life will quit fighting with you when you quit fighting with it!

LEARNING AND LIVING

When your emphasis changes, it is remarkable how differently your life will look. Once you quit wasting time defending yourself and your rightness and begin to embrace life as a learning process that has been designed just for you, challenges will appear before you with potential and purpose. Here is a life approach that I want to encourage you toward. Think about these four words every day. Let them become an outline for your life performance.

1. **Listen**—Expect insights to come in unexpected ways.
2. **Learn**—Live each day with an open heart and an open mind.
3. **Love**—Embrace each life experience with a spirit of thanksgiving.
4. **Lead**—Remember, to whom much is given, much is expected!

Because you have the power to choose how you are going to respond to your life, make the choice now to seize each day with all of your weaknesses and deficiencies. Trust in the security that comes from your personal faith, build relationships that are purposed to encourage and inspire, and be the exception that employers love. Invite critique. Welcome criticism. It will be amazing how quickly you will begin to hear praise replace criticism as your world applauds your performance. When that applause doesn't come or isn't adequate, however, listen for the applause you will hear within yourself and take a bow.

TAKE THE CHALLENGE

Identify three people in your world to seek out to give you a life review. Select people who know you and are committed enough to you to be honest. Try to find people who will be representative of each dimension of your life. Share with them your personal statements of purpose, mission, and vision. Ask them to help you discover the things you are doing that well-represent what you are attempting to sell to your world. Ask them also for their insights as to what you might change. Encourage their criticism. Listen and learn.

AFFIRMATIONS

I am secure in my weakness.
I invite criticism.
I will stay humble no matter what.
I am the student, and life is my teacher.
I will listen for life's lessons.
I will always fail forward.

THE PROFILE
OF A PROFESSIONAL

When you think "professional," who comes to your mind? No doubt it's someone who is not only *proud* of what they do but is also extremely *responsible*. They take responsibility for their performance. I am currently observing someone's professional performance on a very personal level, and as of this moment I am extremely impressed. I say, "as of this moment," because this experience is new to Barbara and me. We recently received a letter from city hall informing us that over the next three weeks there will be extensive work done to the sewer line running across our backyard. It warned that anything impinging upon the utility easement to the property should be moved. So swing set, trampoline, everything had to go. They did say that the contractor involved would be responsible for the yard and anything that they might damage in the process. Their work began with very little intrusion into our property or into our privacy. Unfortunately, that short-lived reality has been exchanged for a seminightmare. We first noticed our toilets stopped working. It then worsened when the sewer began to overflow into our house. Our carpets were damaged and the house was a mess. But that wasn't the end of it. It then got worse as they cut both the cable and the electrical service to our house. That in turn has damaged, or at least negatively affected, our home computer system.

I am not sure where this drama will end, but I will tell you that through it all I've been most impressed with the professional way in which the contractor has responded to this unfortunate series of events. They graciously received our frantic calls, they provided hotel accommodations of our choosing, they immediately deployed people to clean the carpets, and they took responsibility for any repair that might be involved with the computer. They have been clear and committed to the process of returning our yard and our house to its original condition. The point of this personal experience is to applaud the professionalism of this company. Notice that the applause is not for their perfection. The applause is for their responsibility in the process of dealing with their imperfection. Professionals always accept responsibility for their performance; they know there are no excuses. I hope this company continues to maintain their professionalism until the end of this challenging experience. It would be a shame to spoil a great performance.

Professional is a designation you should be able to trust. It is a designation that naturally evokes an almost immediate sense of respect and recognition from most people. When you are in the presence of a professional your expectations are simply higher. You have confidence that you can trust "professionals." After all, you are paying for that kind of performance aren't you? They have identified themselves as being professionals in their field haven't they? What should you expect?

The truth is, *professional* is a label that has become really confusing in today's world. All too easy to assume or acquire, anyone can become a professional in any field by attending some seminar, taking some course, wearing some tag or logging on to some Web site. I just saw two people interviewed on *Good Morning America* who were being recognized as "relationship experts." What does that mean? How did they achieve that status? It just should not be that easy to receive a trust-producing title. We are living in a day when too many claim to be professionals while all too few actually represent the claim.

Years ago there was a distinct separation between the ranks of professionals and amateurs in athletics. Those who accepted money for athletic performances were automatically tagged "professional" and were considered to be advanced performers. In some ways, it was a distinctive title; in other ways, it was restrictive. Olympic competition, once reserved for the great amateur competitors of the world, didn't welcome professionals. And then came "The Dream Team." The very best from the NBA were brought together to produce an unbeatable result. I realize that there was reason for this American response to the way the rest of the world circumvented professional restriction. At one time, being a golf pro was particularly confusing. The great Bobby Jones, an attorney, "professionally speaking," avoided wearing the professional golfer tag although he was the greatest golfer of his time. Golf professionals were actually looked down upon until the likes of Ben Hogan, Sam Snead, and Byron Nelson hit the scene.

So what is it that makes a professional, a professional? What is there about a person deserving of that kind of respect and recognition? Does professionalism reside in some degree achieved or designation that is awarded? What should we expect of those who portray themselves as being professionals in the service they provide, for the product they produce, or for the performance they give? Most people who read this book will be considered professional in one life role or another. In fact, because in our country every person is given tax consideration for the place they occupy, everyone *is* professional on the basis of their "pay for play" life status. Maybe that is the source of so many of our communication challenges. We expect a great deal of one another because we believe we are all being paid on some level to occupy the space we occupy and to do the job we do.

How many times have you gone to someone because of their claimed professional status only to be disappointed in less-than-professional performance? I issue this challenge to those who so proudly wear their professional titles simply because they have completed and achieved some kind of advanced educational degree: Actively and consitently communicate with integrity what you know to the world, who looks to you because of your advertised expertise. Unless you can do that, your so-called professional status is at best irrelevant.

Purposed Performance is a call for professionalism in the most practical sense of the word.

Purposed Performance is a call for professionalism in the most practical sense of the word. It is a plea to those who would claim to be professionals to actually behave like one. It is a challenge to all of us who choose relationship roles in life to approach them with the spirit of a professional. The following progression will take you to a new and challenging place in that regard: "To whom much is given much should be expected." Our response to life's privilege must be professional. It must be on purpose!

PHILOSOPHY: PROUD AND RESPONSIBLE

Professionals are people who strive to be recognized and respected for the role that they play. They take great pride in the preparation they make and for the life performance they give. Their greatest desire is to evoke spontaneous applause from their world. Professionals work hard and want to walk away from what they do feeling happy about their accomplishments. While they are by nature competitive, their most intense competition is always with themselves. True professionals, however, are also quick to recognize and applaud the accomplishments of others. They are just proud to be in the arena.

Professionals take a healthy sense of pride in what they do. To be proud is not always bad. In too many cases, it is automatically regarded as being self-serving. But professionals are proud to wear the name of the role they represent and to be recognized as being distinctively prepared to serve. They expect to be held to higher standards. Always recognizing and playing to an audience, professionals enjoy being showcased. They want their work to be critically analyzed and appreciated. They are not afraid of exposure, because they are proud of their performance.

Purposed performers strive to be professional in every life role. While mediocrity is never satisfactory, don't become defeated by the illusion of perfection. To be professional is not a claim of perfection, but it does represent the constant pursuit of perfection. Pursuing perfection and claiming perfection are two very different things.

> *To be professional is not a claim of perfection, but it does represent the constant pursuit of perfection.*

Think of someone you consider a consummate professional; someone you admire and appreciate. Stay away from the impersonal fantasy of celebrity; keep it personal. The person who comes to my mind is someone I have had the privilege of knowing for over a decade. Though he wears the designation of professional proudly, Tom Dawson epitomizes humility to both his peers and his patients. He constantly works at his dental profession, and at one time, by his own admission, he allowed himself to become obsessive about his work. But with the help of his loving and equally professional wife, Karen, he successfully avoided that abyss. Committed to sharing what he has learned with others, he delights in mentoring those who will ultimately carry on his legacy. He avoids the delusion of blaming others when it is convenient and is quick to applaud the accomplishments of those around him. He is in a field that has rapidly grown to be impersonal and uncaring, yet he and his team model excellence in patient care. Thanks Tom and Karen and company for the show. It is always fun to watch.

Besides being proud and responsible in their pursuits, professionals are also persistent. They don't give up easily. They fight to the very end because of who they are. I admire those professionals who see things through to the end no matter what the sacrifice is to them personally. Several years before my father's death, he had to undergo heart surgery. His surgeon was gracious as he met us and explained the procedure. He did the surgery early one morning. Several hours later we were delighted to hear that all had gone well and that my father should be recovering. Throughout the day we stood by watching and waiting. At about 1 A.M. the next morning, I was awakened by a call from the hospital telling me that my father had taken a turn for the worse and might not make it. I remember returning to the hospital and being met by the same surgeon who had operated on my father that morning. He told me there was leakage around Dad's heart. He made no excuses; he just said he would do his best and we should pray. My dad made it through that surgery and had several years with us before he died. I have always been impressed with that doctor's performance. He was there in the morning, and he was there in the night. He didn't pretend to be perfect, but he was present from the beginning to the end. I would like to tell you that my experience with the medical profession has always gone that way, but unfortunately it has not. I guess maybe that is why I so appreciate a professional when I see one.

Our oldest daughter, Angela, has had more than her share of challenges. At twenty-seven, she has dealt with a number of life's threatening illnesses. One of her most trying has been a degenerative back condition that eventually brought her to surgery. Her insurance company provided her a list of "approved" surgeons, and we felt fortunate that one of the approved seemed to be a very experienced professional. At least that is the way he presented himself. In fact, he led Angela and Barbara to believe that her surgery would be very simple. It was one that he had performed hundreds of times in his career. With great fear and trepidation, we placed our confidence in this professional. When he came to us after the surgery, I could tell from the moment I saw him that something was wrong. He briefly mentioned some "unanticipated" trouble with the nerves in her back but quickly said that he was sure she would recover. That was the last time we had the opportunity to see our "professional." He never came to see Angela after the surgery. Her pain was excruciating, and she was able to get no relief. She literally passed out every time she was forced by well-meaning physical therapy "professionals" to get on her feet. Two years of pain and therapy on various levels later, Angela had to endure a second surgery. This one was corrective in nature. The first doctor had made errors in judgment. Unfortunately, because of his lack of professionalism, Angela has had to be the victim. Had he monitored her situation more closely or even paid closer attention to this "routine" surgery, perhaps her life would have been a little easier these past few years. If we had only been working with a real professional, how different things might have been.

Every role you play deserves your professional attention. You need to be proud of the designation you have achieved. You need to represent well the name that you wear. You need to be responsible for your performance. Claim the victory in success and the opportunity in failure. Above all, be there until the end, no matter what!

PERSPECTIVE: READY AND REPRESENTATIVE

Being professional is a lifestyle to live not a designation to wear. Professionals always approach their challenges with great care. They recognize that nothing can be assumed or taken for granted. In fact, anathema to the professional is familiarity. The moment you begin to take things for granted, that is the moment your performance as a professional will be compromised.

It is important at this point in the discussion to establish the fact that life is not always about performance. You should not always be "on." Time must be taken for rest and for recreation. In these moments, it is vital that you come off stage and, as my girls say, "chill." At least, I think they still say that. Just yesterday, during an employee coaching session for one of the companies with whom I work, a participant asked me if I ever quit "presenting." He specifically wanted to know if my wife ever had to suggest I "get off stage" and just be myself. On one hand, I wanted to quickly defend myself and say that I try desperately to be myself when I am presenting. Understanding, however, the true nature of his question, the answer was definitely yes. Barbara has to remind me occasionally to "lighten up." It is not easy for a guy like me, and I know that I am not alone. On the other hand, never getting on the stage to begin with is worse.

The real key is an understanding of timing. It is in understanding the response being called for by the "moments" in our lives. There is a time in every life role for you to be professional in your response, when you are called upon to do what you know your role calls for and not what you feel. To that degree, I believe there is a sense in which I have a professional role to play as a husband, a parent, a son, a friend, and a citizen just as clearly as the role that I play as a speaker and coach. I must tell you that most of the time it is easier on the more traditional professional life stage. For instance, it is tough to be a parent when you see your child being victimized by someone else's error in judgment. Recently, I had the challenge as a grandparent of sitting directly behind home plate watching an umpire call my granddaughter out on strikes in slow-pitch softball. I have been around the game a long time; I've pitched and I've umpired. Being as objective as I can possibly be, the calls this guy made were ridiculous. I don't know what happened to him, but for a few moments he totally lost sight of the zone, and Savannah had to suffer for his mistake. Now tell me, what do I do? I know what I felt like doing. But instead I just yelled, "Way to go, Savannah!"

In fact, let me tell you what my father would have done. I know because I saw him do it, and it is indelibly imprinted in my memory. I can't tell you how many times as a kid I heard my dad climb an umpire. He would have been up on the screen yelling at the top of his lungs, "You blind goose!" I'm not exaggerating. In fact, he was literally thrown out of a ballpark on one occasion for one of his tirades. I tell you this because, although I love my dad for a lot of things, he got this part wrong. In one sense, he taught me because he modeled something for me that I never wanted to represent to my children or to any children. Some of the most "unprofessional" moments I have ever seen have been around youth athletic competition, and it was a parent who was not playing the role they needed to be playing.

For a number of years I coached a group of sixth grade girls in a YMCA basketball league in our community—one of my great joys. The final year I coached we had a great team. They had worked hard together for a long time, and they had really learned something about the game. They learned to set picks effectively, to get positioned for rebounds. They learned a few offensive sets. I couldn't have asked for a more committed group of girls and parents. In the championship game, they played particularly well and really outperformed the other team. The lopsided score said it all: The other team was not as prepared. After the game, while I was thanking one of the young referees for the job he had done, a parent from the opposing team marched down the bleachers screaming at me, accusing me of teaching my girls dirty tactics and purposefully hurting their girls. I couldn't believe it. The young ref tried to step in and help, and when he did the woman slapped him. Stunned, I was really embarrassed for this woman's poor husband and daughter. Completely irresponsible, that woman really didn't play her parental role well in that moment.

I realize that I am taking some liberty with the word *professional* in this chapter. I know that I am stretching it beyond its normal meaning, but I am doing it on purpose to focus on those times when we are asked to perform outside of how we feel. There are times when we need to "chill" and listen to our bodies and minds as they cry out for rest. There are times to purposefully avoid being "on." I really think that kind of response, however, is the sign of a professional. Real professionals do not burn out because they know how to pace themselves through the challenge.

Remember, anticipation is the best form of preparation. So if you are married, you can know every day that there will be times when you have to function as a professional. You may not feel like getting up and going to work, but you do it, and you do it well because you are responsible. There might be times when the easier thing to do is give up on the marriage. It might not feel good anymore. Yet because of the responsibility you feel in the relationship, you respond and you recover. Just this week I met a man who is married to a woman who has become extremely ill. In fact, she has been that way for a long time. He is not only a provider for the family, but he is the primary caregiver for his life partner. I can tell you that this is a disciplined professional. Maybe you know someone like that, or maybe you are that someone. The really great performances in life are rarely being given on the public stages of the world. They are in the trenches of life. They are taking place where few can see. The real life professionals are quietly and responsibly making life happen one day at a time.

The real life professionals are quietly and responsibly making life happen one day at a time.

Through one of my seminars I met a man who shared a life story that I believe epitomizes professionalism as a parent. I am not saying he and his wife have been perfect, nor would they. Remember, it is the pursuit not perfection that defines the professional. During a corporate training session I was conducting, I asked this group of about seventy-five people for examples of life changes they had made as a result of being exposed to Purposed Performance training. This man spoke up and said that both he and his wife had come to an important place in their relationship with their daughter. He then shared with this group what he and his family had been enduring for the past several years. A few in this group knew and were sensitive to his challenges, while the majority in the room listened with rapt attention as he described nothing less than a parent's nightmare. He said that he and his wife had decided to adopt and raise their nine-month-old granddaughter. Their daughter was a drug addict in her early twenties, living on the street as a prostitute. They had done everything they knew to do to help her make better choices. They had spent all that they had and more in that effort. She had been to recovery facilities and through counseling. They had let her come home on several occasions only to be disappointed as she stole from them and sold their possessions to support her habit. He told this group that he and his wife had now chosen not to allow their daughter to come home until she was well. They would no longer be partners with her in her addiction. They were doing this, he said through tears, not because they felt like it but rather because they were convicted that it was the responsible thing they needed to do as parents. He went on to say that they anticipated that she might have other children and, as a result, they might have other grandchildren come their way. Some might even be "crack" babies. They had decided that they would adopt these children as well and spend their lives giving them life if that became their reality. Once again, he stressed not because they felt like it but because they believed in it. This couple is modeling professional parenting in the moment. I could go on and on about others I have met who model the kind of resilience that would press the very boundaries of any parent. Being the professionals we are called to be as parents might be the toughest challenge of all. It certainly is not for the weak of heart or mind. It takes a professional.

There are other roles in life that call for professional behavior. It is not always easy to be a friend. Sometimes it would be easier to just let go. It is not easy to be a student. There are teachers who make the learning process more difficult than it needs to be. It is not easy to be a volunteer. Too often they become the victims of the very people they are committed to serving. Every relationship in life will press you at times. You have to anticipate it and prepare yourself for it so you won't be surprised when it happens. We are rarely at our best when we are surprised; most often we are reactive. Professionals anticipate and prepare. They also find every opportunity to practice. It is so difficult to prepare and practice for some of the challenges life will throw at you, but we can "mind" through the possibilities every time we have the opportunity. We can practice with those around us who are going through their moments when professionalism is required. We can be with them and learn through them. It is all in the way you see things.

PERFORMANCE: **COMPETITIVE AND COMMITTED**

Professionals are competitive. Where it is called for, they are competitive with others. At all times they are competitive with themselves. Professionals are committed to the role they are playing and embrace the pursuit of excellence even when it is not always achieved. Purposed performers are professionals in the truest sense of the word because they have accepted responsibility for each life role. Once you have chosen the professional path, you are ready for the games to begin.

Being professional in the game of life requires an answer to each of the following questions:

1. What role are you seeking to play?
2. What competition will you face?
3. What can you anticipate?
4. How will you prepare?
5. How accountable will you be?
6. How will you respond to the challenges?

Professionals do not play in games or pursue challenges they are not prepared for. They are in the game they are in on purpose. Many, if not most times, it has come at some cost. So the beginning point has to be one of choice. There can be no role confusion for the professional. Knowing the ground rules becomes vital to the process. Too many people take on roles and responsibilities with no clue as to what will be expected from them. All relational conflicts come as a result of expectations that are confused. So begin by clarifying and committing yourself to the life role you are choosing. Remember, you can always begin again.

Competition is an interesting dynamic in our lives. Some are greatly energized by it while others are paralyzed. The truth is that competition is part of the program for the professional. At the very least, you will be competing with yourself to perform beyond your natural instincts. You will be purposefully pursuing a disciplined course because of the commitment you have made. There will also be the presence of other competitive factors. Sometimes they come in the form of people, but often our greatest competition seems to be against time.

Many times, it will involve keeping score or achieving a particular result. What factors will define and/or impact your performance? You always want to be a student of the competition no matter what form it may take.

Stress is a word that has become all too common in our lives. Once you are clear about the challenge itself and you have identified the competitive factors involved, you are ready to exercise your anticipative skills. What can you expect from your challenges as a professional? Professionals work to reduce the stress involved in the games they play by anticipating the challenges ahead of time and by preparing in advance for wise responses. Much like the golf professional, you need to prewalk your course as much as possible. Surprise is not something you want to build into the game for yourself. To avoid that, survey the challenges and the competitive forces and see ahead of time the things that might be required of you.

Practice makes professional. The greatest distinction between those who are professional and those who are not lies in their commitment to preparation. Years ago, while I was still hitting the tennis ball a lot, I received a call from a guy from my high-school tennis team who had turned professional

Practice makes professional.

after college. He wanted to know if I would meet him at the courts; he needed a practice partner for the day. I quickly said yes thinking that it would be great fun to be back hitting the ball with this guy. What a joke! He almost killed me. We hit the ball for six hours. I was cramping in places I did not even know I could cramp. Practice for this professional was far more serious than the fun expected by this amateur. The point is that playing the role of a professional in any life moment requires preparation that most of us are not making. What preparation are you making for the challenges you can anticipate as a husband? What are you doing to prepare yourself for the role you will be playing as parent to your children? What can you do to prepare for your eventual role as care giver to a parent? What can you do to make yourself more effective for the friends in your life? How much are you preparing, period, in your life? Most people wait until they are required to react. It is natural for life to be done that way. In this arena, natural is not healthy. We don't have to wait until life happens to respond to it. We can respond in advance through anticipation and preparation, and then when the challenge arises we will be ready and confident. Stress will be minimized. Performance will be "professionalized."

Choose to be accountable for your life performances. Create relationships that will help provide the positive tension you need to cross the line of discipline when life moments require it. Begin by getting accountable to yourself. Be specific about how you intend to respond to the challenge that is before you. Write it down. Don't let it become a moving target in your mind's eye. Get as specific as is possible. Where appropriate, go public. It is amazing how much more serious you will become about those things you have committed to others. Relationships are most effective when they become the accountability support you need in order to live your life on purpose. Once again, they are not natural. It is far more natural to be in relationships with people who will sympathize and commiserate with you in your challenge. While empathy is a value we all appreciate in relationships, sympathy might be the last thing we need. We need people who will tell us what we need to hear, not just what we want to hear. Sensitivity is always vital to any relationship, but sensitivity that swells into misplaced sympathy can be destructive or, at best, counterproductive.

Prepare for the challenges you cannot anticipate because they will always be there. In spite of all of your best efforts, you will find yourself facing challenges you are not prepared for. The choice you must premake is not to react. Prepare to ask questions that will give you the bridge time you need to create the response you really want to make. You might ask, "How did we get to this point?" or "What would you do if you were me?" Get comfortable with saying things like, "I don't know what to say. You've caught me off guard. Help me understand more about . . ." The truth is, you can prepare for those unforeseen moments by getting comfortable with the potential for them happening.

Professional performance in life requires intention, doing life on purpose. It does not take place as a reaction to life. It always occurs as a prepared response to life's moments. While instincts will find their way into some of our life responses, professionals realize that their instincts must be conditioned and sharpened by their preparation. Professionals are always ready in the moment: They are calm in the face of chaos, and they are confident because of their condition.

PROFESSIONAL AND PROUD, ON PURPOSE!

You have the choice to make, but I recommend that you "turn professional" in life. You have what it takes. You qualify as a person. The only thing left is for you to purposefully walk onto your life's stage. The only real alternative is for you to choose to live your life as an amateur performer, which means you are not ready to put it on the line. You have some false sense that you can do life as a spectator. Somehow you have reasoned that you can stay in the audience of life. But life's moments will call you out of the stands eventually and onto the stage. Challenges will ultimately legislate that you become more than a spectator. The qualifications for your life roles will demand a professional response sooner or later, so you might as well make the move and get set for your performance. Hopefully, you will choose to take the professional challenge.

TAKE THE CHALLENGE

Choose and identify a specific life role you are presently playing. Then answer the questions listed in the Performance section of this chapter. Consider each question one at a time with a specific life role in mind.

AFFIRMATIONS

I am a professional.
I am preparing for the moment.
I am ready for the challenge.
I am on the stage.
I love the opportunity.
I am confident in my outcome.

THE LEARNING
ADVANTAGE

Can you remember how excited you were to graduate high school? You had finally gotten it done. Twelve long and laborious years of forced learning. Now it was all behind you. Any learning that would go on in the future would be up to you, boy. No one could make you go to college. Going to college would finally be your choice to make, and, if you did choose to go, you would choose which classes you would take and you would choose which classes *you* would attend. Do you remember those days of delusion and denial?

I think perhaps we have become confused and even delusional as a culture about learning because of our mandated and structured education system. Instead of inspiring the spirit of a continuing and growing desire to learn, it seems to have created a great deal of aversion to the learning process. This is not meant to be a shot at teachers. Many dedicated professionals have inspired their students despite the constraints of the very limiting systems. Unfortunately however, too many teachers have not fulfilled their roles professionally and instead have quenched the learning spirit in their students through their arrogance and insecurity, or perhaps just indifference. The point is that somewhere along the line, for some reason, many if not most people have allowed themselves to believe that there would only be so much learning going on for them in this life. Learning would have limits. When we got out of school, whatever that meant to us, we were through with this learning stuff. No more reading for learning purposes. Reading only for amusement and personal entertainment, and only when I am ready.

Do you remember when a person with an undergraduate degree was considered exceptional? I was only the second person on my father's entire side of the family to have attended college and who actually earned a degree. Today, many kids going to college and achieving degrees aren't necessarily the ones learning anything. Many are in denial and avoidance, denying the reality that they have barely even begun to learn anything and are in absolute avoidance about going to work for a wage that they all feel is beneath them. I passionately support continuing education. I am simply opposed to "professional students" who are totally dependant upon others for their support and yet see no prospect for changing their career path in the near future.

When I was a child I learned as a child. When I became an adult I put away childish things. What does that mean? I realize that I have taken liberty with an inspired Scripture to ask this question, but it is a question we each must ask and answer. And the answer we come up with better be the right one. Both our present and our future depend upon it. Is learning an activity for children? Is learning a childish thing that adults ultimately put away? You may think that these questions are pretty childish. In fact they really are, but you should listen to the kind of response I get from many of the adults I challenge to continue to engage and even embrace the learning process.

I am constantly recommending reading as an exercise that, in my opinion, is essential to the fitness required for twenty-first century people. I consistently hear reactions like they are "not into reading." I hear that they don't have the time. They want to know if the reading that I am recommending is mandatory. They want to know if it is something required by the company and if they'll be paid for the time it will take for them to read. I have met educated men and women who claim not to have read a book in the past thirty years. I have actually met high school graduates who say they have never actually completed reading a book, ever. From the reactions I receive from adults in the marketplace, it seems many actually believe they have graduated the need to learn. The answer for them must be that learning is something you put away as an adult.

Today, many are painfully learning that continuing education is not really optional for those who wish to be successful or even endure this century. Many have allowed themselves to depend upon experience as their ongoing professional credential. Unfortunately, yesterday's experience is not being valued nearly as much as tomorrow's potential. Companies are choosing not to build their present or their future upon people who are content with what they already know and, as a result, will resist the changes of tomorrow. You must prove yourself to be someone who is fit for learning things yet to be envisioned and someone who is comfortable with what you do not know. Otherwise, you are of limited value to the marketplace of today. If you are comfortable with those limitations, and/or if you believe those limitations will last you for as long as you intend to go, then good for you. I mean it. Pursue that course. The purpose of this chapter is to heighten your awareness of what you may be avoiding. If you have more future before you than you have credentials to endure it, then you may have some education to pursue. If you have the credentials but you are having trouble making the application or communicating what you know, then you still have a lot to learn in order for what you know to make any real difference. In fact, no matter who you are, even if you are in the "retirement" chapter of life, you have a lot to learn. We all do.

The following progression is meant to provide a positive, productive way to help you proceed in meeting this twenty-first-century challenge. It's meant to provide an advantage to those who choose to embrace it. I encourage you to seize the advantage. Choose to be a child for the rest of your life and never stop learning.

PHILOSOPHY: STRENGTH AND SECURITY

We are now living in a mutually competitive world, and the only competitive advantage any of us will have will be the learning advantage. There was a day when all you needed to do to keep your job was to show up and do it. The only thing you had to do to stay married was to get married. That day is gone. Today, doing a good job may not be good enough. Being a good husband and/or wife

Enthusiasm in the present is directly related to your performance in the future.

may not be enough. You not only have to do your job well, but you have to be constantly learning and preparing for what might be next. You need to be learning and growing as a person in your marriage to be prepared for the challenges that marriage will bring. It's in the spirit of preparation for your next challenge that you'll find the creativity and energy for your performance in your present challenge. Enthusiasm in the present is directly related to your performance in the future. All of us must connect the dots between today's expectations and tomorrow's possibilities in order to create the mindset essential for living in the twenty-first century.

Several years ago, I was invited to speak to a group of several hundred cafeteria workers in a large public school system. The person managing this group wanted me to inspire these people to more personal and professional customer service within their context. I began the session by walking down the middle aisle and asking them this question: "What do you plan to do in your next job?" The response was spontaneous. One woman very quickly reacted on behalf of them all: "What are you talking about?" I told them that if my experience with school cafeterias and the experience of my children were indicative of what was going on in this school district, I would not think their future was very bright. I asked them if they knew how prevalent "outsourcing services" had become in the school cafeteria world.

After explaining what that could mean in their case, they quickly got the point. After assuring them that I was not on some clandestine mission to bring them a message from their employer, we got down to work. I asked them to talk about how they could make things better where they were and, in the process, better prepare themselves for their future. I told them that their future might be right where they were if they worked creatively toward making themselves valuable to the school district and if the district continued to choose them as their answer. Their growth in the present as professionals might also prepare them for a future in some other field. Either way, they needed to be preparing for their future. It was incredible to see just how quickly they got into the flow. The creative and inspirational power of the collective mind is awesome. But in order to become more creative about their future, they had to realize the insecurity of their present.

I recently had a similar experience with a group of employees who were really not happy with the way things were going in their organization. Several people within the group had watched as some of their coworkers, long-term employees, lost their jobs. They were really dealing with a sense of grief much like postwar trauma victims experience. Wondering if they would be next, they were generally unenthusiastic and unhappy as a group about a number of things. I put them into small groups and asked them to work in those groups as though they were distinct and individual teams. I challenged them to respond to the following scenario: "Within the next year, sooner than later, probably half of the team you are working with will not be around. How do you respond today to what you now know, with some degree of certainty, about tomorrow?" Reaction was almost immediate: "We will sue the bastards." I told them that they could certainly pursue that course if they chose, but they must work through that strategy as a team and deal with the ramifications of that response.

Someone else suggested that the best thing to do would be to get drunk. Once again, I affirmed that course as a potential strategy but that I wanted them to work through the challenges and make sure it would take them in the direction they really wanted to go. Others replied that they would just take another job.

Again, I recognized that idea as being possible as long as it accomplished their purpose. One guy, who really was a lot of fun, said, "I think I will just be a motivational speaker." I told him that I thought he would make a great one. I just challenged him to discuss in his group how he might get paid for one of his performances and to determine just who it would be that would pay him.

After about ten minutes of reaction, I cut them loose as groups to come up with their team's response. The insight of the group was amazing. After getting through the emotion of the beginning, they got down to proactive and creative responses to their challenge. They came up with a number of things they could do in the present if they had to face that reality. Continued learning was consistently part of the answers they discovered. We then discussed just how real that exercise was for all of us. What they had developed as an imagined response should, in fact, become their actual performance. I really hope that it does.

Most people today are completely dependent upon their jobs for both their livelihood and their emotional stability, whereas the organizations they work for have no such commitment. It is not good business for organizations to make commitments to people that they are not committed to keep. It is likewise not good business for people to depend upon commitments that have never been made and which will eventually not be kept. Professional security will always be a product of personal growth and development. It is your ever-increasing value that will keep you secure in today's marketplace.

It is your ever-increasing value that will keep you secure in today's marketplace.

The same is true in your personal life. Too many people depend on their spouses for both their livelihood and emotional stability. Yet they are doing little to strengthen and grow their marriages. It is important to live every day in the moment, and every moment presents opportunity for you to learn something that can strengthen you for tomorrow.

If you have been around long and have been paying attention, you realize just how quickly life can change. The people you love most cannot guarantee you their presence tomorrow. Misplaced dependency can be personally destructive. It's so important for you to be preparing now for the strength that might be required of you tomorrow. Years ago, I counseled a young woman who was engaged to be married. During one of our sessions she said that she loved her fiancé so much and that she could not even think about living without him. I told her that she had better do just that before she got any further into this relationship, because even after they were married she might be called upon to live life without him. He could not be her security; he did not qualify. No human being does. Just recently I've been reminded of that human reality again through a dramatic and tragic turn of events not too far from where I live. A Houston, Texas, father recently had to deal with the burial of his five children, and with his mentally ill wife being responsible for their deaths. One day he had a wife, five children, and a seemingly prosperous and happy existence. The next day he had lost it all. I am encouraged by the way he has handled this very public tragedy. He has been very clear about the fact that his strength comes from the faith that he has placed in a loving, merciful God. You might not be able to wrap your mind around his response to this tragedy. You probably don't have to right now, and hopefully, you never will. But I do hope that you and I will prepare in such a way as to have that same strength when our life challenges come.

Continued learning will be your only advantage. You must consistently prepare and strengthen every dimension of your life. The preparation you make and the strength you receive today may well be the source of your security tomorrow.

PERSPECTIVE: AWARE AND AWAKE

Letting go of any misplaced dependency upon what you think you know will create for you an entirely new vision for living. Think about it. If you consider the things you are depending upon today as being things that might very well be gone tomorrow, how differently will your world look? One thing you can depend

upon is that what you think you know today will probably be meaningless tomorrow. Change is the one thing
you can trust.

Change is the one thing you can trust.

Years ago, I began in the mortgage banking field as a
trainee. Given the opportunity to learn from the ground up, I
remember spending hours upon hours typing FHA and VA loan
applications on an IBM typewriter. They had to look good, so I expertly used
correction tape and Liquid Paper to deal with my mistakes. Once typed, they
were put into the mail for an underwriter to consider. Today, my prowess in
typing applications on a typewriter and correcting them would be lost in the
mortgage-lending business. Everything is computerized. Corrections are automatic. Submissions are online and in real time. My typing skills have been
valuable to me in this computer age, but many of the other mechanics I mastered are irrelevant. If I were to be successful today in that field, it would not
be based upon what I knew yesterday. My success today would be a product of
what I would be learning. My experience would have value, but it would not
be valuable enough to keep me competitive in today's marketplace. I have to
continue developing value as a professional, or I will miss valuable opportunity
that the future will provide. You will too.

I was raised in a Christian home with Christian parents, but we didn't go to
church a lot. I knew a lot about God. We sang about Jesus and his love. I thought
I knew what I believed. It was natural for me to assume the faith of my parents.
Then came college days. I was confronted with my mortality for the first time
during those first few years. Living through them was a miracle in itself. My
search for a personal faith became much more relevant to me during that time. I
grew, however, through those challenging experiences, and I came to a new and
more personal place in my relationship with God. I thought I had it altogether.

Then came my early years as a young professional. I discovered that my post-
college faith was of little value in meeting my present-day challenges. I was once
again brought to my knees in search of a relevant and meaningful walk with God.

I could go on and on about the last twenty years of my life. But suffice it to say, I have continued to pursue a course of learning that shows me there is always more for me to learn about my relationship with God. The most meaningful thing I have learned is that my relationship with him is not contingent upon me. It is based in him. I feel like I am beginning again every day in my faith walk, but I am secure today in the reality that I will spend the rest of eternity learning more about that relationship. In many ways having the accepting faith of a child is my life's ambition. On the other hand, I have to continue to be alert and alive to the new things God wants me to learn every day or I will miss them. You will too.

Physical fitness is another personal challenge that has changed for me. I never used to know that it was a challenge. It just came naturally. I did not even know how to spell *cholesterol* when I was twenty, but I sure do today. In fact, I have had to succumb to the use of medication in order to control my cholesterol level. Exercise was never really difficult for me. Even when it was hard, I always loved it. But somewhere around forty, my body changed its mind. I not only don't like it today, there are many days when I really hate it. When I was playing tennis in college, I had to keep a refrigerator full of weight-supplement drinks to keep my weight up. Trust me, that's not my problem today. I used to hate fish. Today, I actually order it on purpose—even sushi! Hopefully, you are getting the picture. What I knew yesterday about my personal health is irrelevant to my physical condition today. I have to continue to be a student of my own physical health or I will be a victim of my own ignorance and apathy. You will too.

By now you know my family. Barbara and I are life partners. I can't tell you how much she has meant to me and my development as a person. I believe it would be safe to say, however, that neither of us could have imagined what life would hold for us over thirty years ago when we decided to get married. We have gone through chapters in our marriage that I didn't even know existed. It has been a constant course of learning, and the course is not over. It has just begun. The relational quality of the rest of our lives depends upon what we are learning today. Yours does too.

Being a parent, a son, a friend, who would think that those relationships would be so difficult? They all seem so natural—they were supposed to have just happened. I look back on my life, and I cannot believe the things that have gone on in the lives of my children. There have been days when I've thought that if I had known back then what I know today about the challenges of raising children, I'm not sure I would have been so eager to have them. Those are the bad days. The truth is, I would not change one thing about my girls. They have been and are a constant blessing to my life. God has used them to teach me so much about his love. My children are my teachers. When I listen I learn. You will too.

Being a son has had its ups and its downs. There have been days when I wondered why God gave me these parents anyway. Those have been the bad days. The reality is that I more often have wondered why I deserved to have these two people who were willing to devote their lives to me. I have been so loved. They taught me through their sacrifice and commitment. Today, I am being taught even more about the measure of that love and commitment as I am being challenged to love my mother through the last few chapters of her life on this earth. I realize today that I have something to learn from my parents for as long as I live on this earth, even if they leave before I do. You do too.

Friends have always been around for me. We were either in school together or we played ball together. Now I am out of school and I am not playing ball anymore. Now they have to be made. They don't just happen. I have learned that in a lifetime there will be many friends who will come and go, and they will be special, but there will only be a few who will be a consistently invested part of my life. I am learning through my friends just how easy it is to insulate myself from the world. Building good friendships is teaching me a lot about life. They will teach you too.

Life is about learning. Look around you. The relationship you have to this life in all its dimensions is like an ongoing seminar. Living and learning need to be synonymous terms in your vocabulary in order to have the advantage of seeing the world as it really is.

PERFORMANCE: LOVING AND LEARNING

You should never make life choices out of a fear of what you might lose. Rather, you should always live each day with a passion for what you have to gain. The fact that life is constantly changing will either keep you living in a personal grief of sorts about what you perceive you are losing, or it will inspire in you an urgent passion for living life with

> *You should never make life choices out of a fear of what you might lose.*

a confidence that there will always be something new for you to learn and discover. Doing life on purpose is about living life with passion for the people you love and the things you have yet to learn.

You need accountability in your life if you ever hope to achieve the learning advantage you need in today's world. Journaling can serve as a learning gauge of sorts for you. It can monitor your motivation and can be your own personal school. You can keep a finger on the pulse of your heart and mind if you are staying in touch with what you are learning. It's a way for you to be in healthy competition with yourself. If you choose to use it, journaling will provide a basis for meaningful conversation with yourself. Learning needs to become a matter of personal integrity if it will ever become a purposed reality for your life.

What are you learning about your relationship with God? To learn and grow spiritually is a desire I hear spoken from the hearts of people throughout the world. I believe that most people think spiritual growth is something that will just happen to you. While God is clearly the foundation for any spiritual growth you will experience, he will not make changes in you that are not a product of your spiritual choosing. I believe that he will even provide the inspiration, insight, and energy for your pursuit. You, however, will have to choose to join him in the journey. God is speaking every day in the world around you. He is in the big picture, and he is in the details. It is like there is a constant workshop going on, and he is the leader. I have to tell you that there are days when I would like to be given a pass. I believe that God knows my capacity and is merciful in providing both pass and protection when he believes it to be in my best interest. I believe, however, that I have to be tuned in more often than not, or I am probably not going to know what is going on. It is like skipping algebra classes for a semester and then being tested over what you missed. Life can be like that. I think it is important for me to live every day with a conscious determination to learn something that will strengthen and prepare me for the days to come.

What are you learning from you? You spend more time with yourself than with any other person in this life. Yet, you probably spend less quality time with you than any other person in this life. The majority of the time you spend with yourself is probably reactive. You spend a lot of time dealing with yourself on the basis of what is wrong or on what needs to improve. You are in almost constant comparative analysis. It's important to grow in your relationship with you and to listen to what your body is saying. Plug all your energy leaks. Let exercise become as much your regimen as eating is. Plug all your emotional leaks. Emotional support through coaching or counseling can help you gain the insight necessary to make your personal adjustments. The point is that you are the only one who can ultimately take care of you. Others can provide insight and support, but you are the one who will make the choices and changes that must be made.

What are you learning from and through the people in your life? Learning through life relationships will not just happen. You must be invested every day in the people around you in order to maximize your personal growth potential through those relationships. Much like spiritual growth, you can't afford to miss too many classes and still be ready to deal with the tests that are definitely coming. You can't afford to wait until the kids are out of the house to start working on your marriage. By then, the person you married will be a stranger. You can't keep putting off time with kids and expect to experience them at a more convenient time. The time you are putting off today will be opportunity that will not exist tomorrow. The moment you can share with a parent who needs your love and attention today will probably not exist for you in that same way tomorrow. The days are dwindling and the hourglass for them will soon be empty.

What are you learning from your professional team? I believe the professional dimension of your life in many ways is the showcase of your life. It is your life expression. Through what you do, you can experience a healthy sense of pride in who you are. I don't believe that the title you wear or the professional role you play should represent the sum and substance of who you are. Titles and roles can change. Your personal performance in the work you do, whatever it is or whatever it is called, is your personal choice and responsibility. I also believe that it can provide a constant source of energy for you as a person if you pay attention to the signals. If you are passionate about learning, you will be able to listen responsively to the criticism offered by your managers, your customers, or your colleagues. They might not be right all of the time, but they will be real. They are there and they are the people you need to achieve success. They are your team; learn from them.

Learning is not an option, really. You will learn from this life in one way or the other. The question is, will you be doing it on purpose or will it be happening to you as a victim? The choice is yours.

ACHIEVING THE LEARNING ADVANTAGE

Tiger Woods was once asked by a well-meaning reporter this question: "Would you rather compete as the underdog and from behind or as the favorite and the one with the lead?" His response was immediate and succinct: "There is no question. I always want to be in the lead. I want others chasing me." I think learning puts you in the lead in life. I believe it will give you an advantage that can be achieved in no other way. The learning I am talking about must be holistic and relationally based to make any real difference. It requires an awareness of your personal need to listen to the world around you and the world within you and requires a commitment to new input. You must become passionate

Purposed Performance is about becoming a scavenger for the advantage.

about your desire to be exposed to new and fresh thought. Purposed Performance is about becoming a scavenger for the advantage. You must be committed to learning as a lifestyle. Once you make this choice, your life will never be the same. Remember, you always have the power to begin again.

TAKE THE CHALLENGE

For the next thirty days, keep a journal. Take a few minutes each day to identify the things that you are learning with God, with yourself, your family, your friends, and your professional team. Remember this is about what you are learning, not about what someone else needs to learn. Keep it personal. If it works for thirty days, you might consider making your journal your new best friend.

AFFIRMATIONS

I am eager to learn.
I will listen and learn from God.
I will listen to and learn from the people in my world.
I am getting stronger every day.
I will keep the advantage.
I value my life, and I will not take it for granted!

CROSSING THE LINE!

Doing life on purpose requires an understanding of life's progression. It all begins with how and what you think. Your philosophy creates a mindset and vision of your world. It becomes your perspective. Your perspective then results in your life response, or reaction. Life performance is always the bottom line. What you think leads to what you see, which results in what you do. It is that simple, yet that complex.

If you believe in your freedom to choose, you embrace power that can never be wrested from you. You see life with a sense of "response-ability." You do not ever have to be a victim unless you choose that course. And why would you ever choose a victim's course if you have a choice in the matter?

If you believe that people are your purposed companions, you will take them more seriously. You will have a deeper sense of respect for the people in your life that will result in a more meaningful vision of life's relationship. You will both recognize and respond to them as a gift meant especially to complement your life. You will also see and respond to them as though you are meant to be a special complement to theirs.

If you believe that communication is an essential connection with the people in our world, then you will approach the challenge with a deeper sense of resolve. You will see the people in your world through eyes intent upon discovery and development. You will become far more interested in what others are saying and far less in what you have to say.

If you believe that conflict has a creative power that is purposed in your life, you will see your daily relational choices as a force to embrace and not avoid. You will approach life's conflicts with great respect, mastering each conflict because of your confidence in the bonding strength it represents.

If you believe that selling is a daily lifestyle, you will see opportunity in every moment to sell the world what you represent. You will be able to present yourself and your mission with purposeful passion. Your life presentations will take on an integrity that only conviction can produce.

If you believe that team is a reality in your life, you will begin to recognize your relationships as being mutually valuable—as being essential to the life you are choosing to live. You will begin to live each day with a new commitment to the success of the people on your life team because you know that their success will be synonymous with your own.

If you believe that life is about serving others, you will humbly approach each day with a keen sense of purpose. You will see the people in your world as people you have been called to serve. You will see people with eyes of attentiveness and will accept the challenges people present as a purpose statement for your life. You will prepare yourself to be there for them, whether they deserve it or not.

If you believe that you are worth it, you will embrace yourself with a determined sense of respect. You will see yourself as being your greatest asset and will become more focused upon the impact you are allowing life to have upon you. You will begin to live life responsively and will pay attention to each dimension of your life as though your life were depending on it.

If you believe that perfection is something that you pursue but will never achieve, you begin to engage each day with a greater sense of confidence. You will see each day as a day to experience and not to conquer. You will recognize each defeat as a victory in progress. You will want to be in the moment because fear will no longer be in your path. What do you have to lose?

If you believe that being professional is a calling that you must accept, you will take each day as a challenge and a chance. You will see the challenge in choosing the road less traveled, and you will see the chance to earn the applause of your world with you leading the way. You will approach each life relationship with a determination to earn the trust that your designation suggests. After all, you are a professional.

If you believe that learning is the only competitive advantage you can gain in this life, you will seize upon every learning opportunity that comes your way. You will see life through eyes of curiosity. You will approach each day as though you were on a mission of discovery. You will read. You will listen. You will learn.

Doing life on purpose is a matter of progression. It is a matter of conviction. May God bless you on your journey.

RECOMMENDED READING

Arbinger Institute. *Leadership and Self-Deception* (Berrett-Koehler Publishers).

Beckwith, Harry. *Selling the Invisible: A Field Guide to Modern Marketing* (Warner Books).

Beckwith, Harry. *The Invisible Touch: The Four Keys to Modern Marketing* (Warner Books).

Berry, Leonard. *Discovering the Soul of Service: The Nine Drivers of Sustainable Business Success* (Free Press).

Bettger, Frank. *How I Raised Myself from Failure to Success in Selling* (Simon & Schuster).

Blanchard, Kenneth and Sheldon Bowles. *Raving Fans: A Revolutionary Approach to Customer Service* (William Morrow & Co.).

Brady, Shelly. *Ten Things I Learned from Bill Porter* (New World Library).

Collins, Jim. *Good to Great* (HarperCollins).

Cooper, Robert K. *The Other 90%: How to Unlock Your Vast Untapped Potential for Leadership and Life* (Crown Publishers).

Covey, Stephen. *First Things First: To Live, to Love, to Learn, to Leave a Legacy* (Fireside).

Covey, Stephen. *The 7 Habits of Highly Effective People* (Simon & Schuster).

Crum, Thomas F. *The Magic of Conflict* (Touchstone).

Frankl, Viktor. *Man's Search for Meaning* (Beacon Press).

Gladwell, Malcolm. *The Tipping Point: How Little Things Can Make a Big Difference* (Back Bay Books).

Jones, Laurie Beth. *Teach Your Team to Fish: Using Ancient Wisdom for Inspired Teamwork* (Crown Publishers).

Jones, Laurie Beth. *The Path: Creating Your Mission Statement for Work and for Life* (Hyperion).

Lencioni, Patrick. *The Five Dysfunctions of a Team: A Leadership Fable* (Jossey-Bass).

Mandino, Og. *The Greatest Salesman in the World* (Bantam Books).

Marcum, Dave, Steve Smith, Mahan Khalsa. *BusinessThink: Rules for Getting It Right—Now, and No Matter What!* (John Wiley & Sons).

Maxwell, John C. *Developing the Leader Within You* (Thomas Nelson).

Maxwell, John C. *Failing Forward: How to Make the Most of Your Mistakes* (Thomas Nelson).

McGinnis, Alan Loy. *The Balanced Life: Achieving Success in Work & Love* (Augsburg Fortress Publishers).

Peck, M. Scott. *The Road Less Traveled* (Simon & Schuster).

Peck, M. Scott. *The Road Less Traveled & Beyond* (Simon & Schuster).

Pelzer, Dave. *Help Yourself: Finding Hope, Courage, and Happiness* (Plume).

Riley, Pat. *The Winner Within: A Life Plan for Team Players* (Berkley Publishing Group).

Rotella, Robert. *Life Is Not a Game of Perfect: Finding Your Real Talent and Making It Work for You* (Simon & Schuster).

Steinberg, Leigh. *Winning With Integrity: Getting What You Want Without Selling Your Soul* (Time Books).

Waitley, Denis. *Empires of the Mind: Lessons to Lead and Succeed in a Knowledge-Based World* (Quill).